THE LIFE OF
BISHOP RICHARD WHATCOAT

By
SIDNEY BENJAMIN BRADLEY

First Fruits Press
Wilmore, Kentucky
c2016

The Life of Bishop Richard Whatcoat. By Sidney Benjamin Bradley.

First Fruits Press, ©2016

Previously published by the Pentecostal Publishing Company, ©1936.

ISBN: 9781621715177 (print) 9781621715184 (digital) 9781621715191 (kindle)

Digital version at http://place.asburyseminary.edu/firstfruitsheritagematerial/123/

Bradley, Sidney Benjamin.

The life of Bishop Richard Whatcoat / by Sidney Benjamin Bradley.
Wilmore, Kentucky : First Fruits Press, ©2016.
198 pages.: illustrations, portraits; 21 cm.
Reprint. Previously published: Louisville, Kentucky : Pentecostal Publishing Company, ©1936.
ISBN: 9781621715177 (paperback)

1. Whatcoat, Richard, 1736-1806. 2. Methodist Church -- Bishops -- Biography. I. Title.

BX8495.W58 B7 2016

Cover design by Jonathan Ramsay

asburyseminary.edu
800.2ASBURY
204 North Lexington Avenue
Wilmore, Kentucky 40390

First Fruits
THE ACADEMIC OPEN PRESS OF ASBURY SEMINARY

First Fruits Press
The Academic Open Press of Asbury Theological Seminary
204 N. Lexington Ave., Wilmore, KY 40390
859-858-2236
first.fruits@asburyseminary.edu
asbury.to/firstfruits

RICHARD WHATCOAT
This portrait of Whatcoat was made of him three years before
coming to America as a missionary

THE LIFE OF

BISHOP RICHARD WHATCOAT

By

Sidney Benjamin Bradley B. D., M. A., Th. M;

PENTECOSTAL PUBLISHING COMPANY,
Louisville, Kentucky.

DEDICATED TO
The two hundredth anniversary of the birth of
Richard Whatcoat

INTRODUCTION.

Richard Whatcoat has long impressed me as being one of the neglected heroes of early American Methodism. He was fortunate in his personal relations to Bishops Coke and Asbury—and especially to the latter. But he was somewhat overshadowed by both of them. Even as Barnabas was more or less concealed by St. Paul, so was Whatcoat hidden by the Asbury to whom he was truly devoted. When the time came that our Church printed some tiny classic volumes about our Pioneers, Richard Whatcoat was not included. If this exclusion may have harmonized with his modesty, it certainly does not represent complete justice.

He arrived in America too late to win a place as a foremost pioneer. The Revolution was past when in 1784 Whatcoat came from England in company with Bishop Coke,—being then 48 years of age. He had but few brief pastorates,—being kept in the office of Presiding Elder until his election as General Superintendent. After sixteen years of such service he came into the Episcopal office when he was sixty-four years old. He served only six years as a Bishop, dying in 1806. Even in that brief period he was often ill, and much hindered in his good work. So unlike Asbury, he did not have the first chance, or the long chance.

It is possible that he was elected Bishop because his gentleness made him the strongest candidate against the vigorous, and sometimes turbulent, Jesse Lee. They were tied on the first ballot; but on the second voting Whatcoat was chosen by 59 ballots as against 55 for Lee.

4

Nathan Bangs intimates that there was no adequate portrait of Whatcoat. The one in the Gallery at the Book Concern Building in New York City is often mistaken for that of a woman. Evidently it does not show him as he was. The meagre biographies do not present him as a half-way charater, while his long travels and his cheerfully borne hardships mark him as a man of strength.

It is my assured judgment that Whatcoat should be rescued from his comparative obscurity. In a sense he was a buffer Bishop standing between Coke and Asbury, and the noticeable William McKendree. Yet he did his part in wondrous faithfulness, never seeking prominence and commending himself everywhere by his kindly and courteous demeanor. Doubtless, he served that early Methodism by giving an example of an Episcopacy more gentle than that of the properly autocratic Asbury! At any rate, Whatcoat died in the love of the Church, and passed triumphantly into the nearer love of the Christ whom he served so signally.

So let us all hail the worthy effort of Reverend Bradley to set a good man on a deserved pedestal in our Methodist Hall of Fame; and let us rejoice that this exemplar of the patience and meekness of Christ comes again to effective repute.

Cordially,

EDWIN HOLT HUGHES.

Bishop Edwin Holt Hughes
Senior Bishop of the Methodist Episcopal Church
Bishop of the Washington Area,
Washington, D. C.

CONTENTS

THE LIFE OF BISHOP RICHARD WHATCOAT
CHAPTER I.

HISTORICAL SETTING

Some lives glow with the brilliancy of the noonday sun and others fade into obscurity with the lengthening shadows of time. Richard Whatcoat is one of the neglected men of Methodism whose sterling virtues has shone with the radiance of a Christian Saint. Early American Methodism will never be complete until Whatcoat has been given his rightful heritage. It is the purpose of this work to place him beside his contemporaries within the historical setting of his time.

The environment is the eighteenth century England. The scene is the parish of Quinton, Gloucestershire County. The surroundings have inspired Poets to sing of their beauty. Without difficult we roam in our imagination with them amid the quaint scenes of Old England. Here an unknown poet describes Whatcoat's nativity in the following words:

From various springs divided waters glide,
In different colours roll a different tide;
Murmur along their crooked banks awhile,
At once they murmur, and enrich the isle,
Awhile distinct, thronged many channels run,
But meet at last, and sweetly flow in one:
There joy to lose their long distinguished names,
And make one glorious and immortal! Thames.

Whatcoat's boyhood was spent not far from "Cooper's Hill." We can easily surmise that Whatcoat often climbed to the summit of "Cooper's Hill" that his soul might be enraptured with the beauty of the surrounding country. No doubt, he could have said many times with Sir John Denham that:

My eye, descending from the hill, surveys
Where Thames among the wanton valleys strays.
Thames, the most loved of all the ocean's sons
By his old sire, to his embraces run,
Hasting to pay his tribute to the sea,
Like mortal life to meet eternity.

The parish of Quinton was located in this lovely country of Gloucestershire through which the "immortal Thames" flowed. It was in such scenes that Whatcoat grew to reach young manhood. Here he worked and played among the:

Woods, meadows, hamlets, farms,
Spires in the vale and towers upon the hills
The great chalk quarries glaring through the shade,
The pleasant lanes and hedgerows, and those homes
Which seemed the very dwellings of content
And peace and sunshine.

This was a great moment in the history of England. The background was radiant with the victories and glories of the past. A new day seems to be dawning. The Revolution of 1688, which banished the last of the Stuart kings and called William of Orange to the throne, marked the end of the long conflict for political liberty in England. Now came the birth of political freedom, exemplified in the "Bill of Rights" and the "Toleration Act" of 1689. Political theories were energetically discussed in an effort to improve government. Moral and social reforms are needed. In order to accomplish these ends, votes were necessary; and to get votes the people of England must be approached with ideas, facts, arguments and information. In 1695 the freedom of the press was realized. Thus printing was seen in a new form in England; the publication of the first daily newspaper, "The Daily Courant," appears in London in 1702. Literature in its widest sense, including the book, the newspaper and the magazine, became the chief instrument of a nation's progress.

The century welcomes Queen Anne to the throne in 1702. Then in rapid succession the Georges follow. The first half of the eighteenth century was characterized by the rapid social development of England. The coming of political freedom to England was not without its contemporaries. Hitherto men had been dominated by the narrow, isolated standards of the Middle Ages. Now for the first time they set themselves to the task of learning the art of living together, while still holding different opinions. Lecky, the historian, tells us that in a single generation nearly two thousand public coffee-houses, each a center of sociability, sprang up in London alone, and the number of private clubs was quite as astonishing.

S. D. McDonnell says, in his "History of the American Episcopal Church," that:

The condition of society which he confronted was one which would have appalled a man not sustained by a profound belief in God's presence with him. At the middle of the eighteenth century, England touched probably the lowest moral and religious point in her history. During more than a century she had been steadily drained of her most vigorous life. The Puritan emigration had carried away tens of thousands of her children whose religion, if hard and gloomy, was at any rate real. The deportation of the Quakers had emptied England of enthusiasm. The old Elizabethan Churchmanship was withdrawn into the secluded haunts of the non-jurors. The most virile and wholesome of her children had long since gone to the New World. What was left was inert, conventional, weak, helpless, like a depleted system, to resist the inroads of miasma. The miasma had already risen in the form of the cold and barren deism which then possessed the popular mind. Shaftesbury, Bolingbroke, Hume, and Tyndal were the teachers who had the public ear. The sordid, debauching reign of the Georges had been established, and its results had begun to show. The moralities, the very decencies of life, were forgotten. Blasphemy became the mark of a gentleman. To "swear like a lord" was the height of the commoner's ambition. New and strange oaths showed a fertile wit. Gambling was the serious business of the court, and the unconcealed recreation of the people. Hogarth shows the fine gentleman meditating suicide after being ruined at play, and the street gamins playing at chuck-farthing on the flat tombstones of St. Paul's Church-yard. Gin was invented, and the street-signs announced unblushingly, that the passer-by could get 'drunk for a penny, drunk, with clean straw, for twopence.' The lubricity of the age matched its frivolity. Most of its literature is now, happily unreadable. Fielding, Smollett, and Sterne have not been able even by their genius to rescue it from its dirt. In a literature where Tom Jones, Peregrine Pickle, Roderick Random, and Tristram Shandy are the best, what must the worst be? Montesquieu says of the English of that day, 'They have no religion.' The age's own judgment of itself appears in the proposal of a parliamentary bill, offered half in jest, and wholly in earnest, 'that the word 'not' should be struck out where it occurs in the Commandments, and inserted in the Creeds!'

This new social life made its mark upon the culture of the eighteenth century, as revealed in the biographies of Johnson, Goldsmith and Burns. The typical Londoner of Queen Anne's day was rude and vulgar in his tastes. The city was filthy, the streets unlighted and infested at night by bands of rowdies and thieves. Men sought to refine their manners according to prevailing standards; a man's first duty was to be elegant and to possess good form, whether he entered society

or a career in literature. One can hardly read a book
or poem of the age without feeling this superficial ele-
gance. Government still had its opposing Tory and
Whig parties, and the Church was divided into Catholics, Anglicans, and Dissenters; but the growing social
life offsets many antagonisms, producing at least the
outward impression of peace and unity. Nearly every
writer of the age turned to religion as readily as to
politics for his theme; the scientific Newton was as
truly religious as the Churchman Barrow, and the
philosophical Locke was no less sincerely religious than
the Evangelical Wesleys. Practically all tempered
their zeal with moderation, and argued from reason
and Scripture. The tendency of the age was definitely
toward toleration. Man found himself in the long
struggle for personal liberty; now he turned to the
task of discovering his neighbor, of finding in Whig
and Tory, in Catholic and Protestant, in Anglican and
Dissenter, the same general human characteristics that
he found in himself. These ends were aided by the
spread of education and by the growth of the national
spirit, following the victories of Marlborough on the
Continent. In the midst of all these confusing elements was needed only a word—Gibraltar, Blenheim,
Ramillies or a poetic Addison to reveal a patriotic people that despite many differences were all alike—Englishmen.

Yet all these new movements in politics, society,
and religion were not unaware of the evils of the age.
For the eighteenth century had brought to light the
sins and worldliness of the Church, and had exposed
the brutal manners and corrupt morals of a great
nation. The Church and the nation, on the threshold
of great wealth and power, had dropped almost to their

lowest depths. For outside her own borders three great men—Clive in India, Wolfe on the plains of Abraham, Cook in Australia and the Islands of the Pacific—were unfurling the flag of St. George over the untold wealth of new lands, and spreading the British Empire world-wide. At home this great and powerful nation was tottering and faltering for the lack of spiritual power. The fame and eloquence of the English pulpit had passed for the time. The Church had lost her power as a messenger for God. The sermons had become essays and her ministers sportsmen. She was without the evidence of the presence of Christ. Truly the fields were ripe for harvest. Who were to be the reapers?

McConnell states that:

Church abuses kept pace with civil ones. A few rich and favored clergy monopolized the livings, and left the mass of the clergy to eke out a miserable livelihood by questionable services to godless patrons, or as 'Fleet parsons.' The clergy were held in popular contempt, and were content to be so. A mitre was schemed for, bribed for, begged for, without sense of shame. When obtained it was prized for the earthly honor it brought, and not for the duty it entailed. Bishops visited their dioceses when it comported with their more serious duties at court. A Welsh bishop who held his see for years never saw it in his life. Confirmations, infrequently held, brought together the young people from miles around for a debauch. Thackeray violates no probabilities when he presents the Bishop of Bath and Wells bowing and smirking in the pump-room before the painted, patched, and powdered old Duchess of Yarmouth, the king's mistress. What was not probable in a church in which the man who 'wept over a dead donkey and left his own mother to starve' received preferment for his 'Sentimental Traveller'? The Church in that century had great men, great schol-

ırs, great bishops, but they pursued their work and
ived their lives apart from the people.   Warburton,
Chillingworth, Butler, Waterland, and Sherlock have
eft their mark upon the generations since, but failed
:o redeem the one in which they lived.   This was the
England which the newly converted Wesley and his
:o-worker Whitefield confronted.   What could be done
with it?   How could it be brought to a sense of God
and to righteousness of life?

The Wesleys and Whitefield had answered the call
and their voices had been heard penetrating the strong-
holds of evil.   Dawn was ushering in a new day spir-
itually.   The light of the new day was to pierce beyond
the veil and shadows of a materialistic age and to bring
hope to weary travellers.   All the Churches of England
were feeling the quickening power of that tremendous
spiritual revival known as Methodism, brought about
by the preaching of Wesley and Whitefield.   Great and
mighty works were being wrought by faith and prayer.

The following story told of a man "kneeling at
work" illustrates this point: "A clergyman observing
a poor man by the road breaking stones with a pickax,
and kneeling to get at his work better, made the re-
mark, 'Ah! John, I wish I could break the stony hearts
of my hearers as easily as you are breaking those
stones.'   The man replied, 'Perhaps Master, you do
not work on your knees.' "

The truth of the story illustrates the difference between the preaching of the average Churchman sermon and the sermons of the so-called Methodists.   The
new prophets of the eighteenth century had learned
this secret, as they went from their knees to the pulpit.
Men were spell-bound and lifted out of sin into a birth
of freedom as their "hearts of stone" melted under
the preaching of the Gospel.

Viewing Methodism from this background, we must agree that it was the natural response of the human soul, to the moral and spiritual destitution of England. This condition is revealed by any reliable historians of this period. Even an extreme Tory author such as Francis Hickman, who wrote in a spirit of hostility, acknowledged that the "Church of England had sunk into a torpor from which it was necessary that it should be aroused."

The very nature of the Anglican church was but a compromise between Roman Catholicism and Protestantism, due to the partial reforms of Henry VIII, "Moderately Protestantized by Edward VI, Catholicized again by Mary, restored to a middle position by Elizabeth, Catholicized by Charles I, abolished by the Commonwealth, brought back to the Elizabethan condition by Charles II, touched up again in the Catholic direction by James II and Anne, amid fierce protests and commotions." One is aware of the fact that any religious enthusiasm would be considered as the deadliest sin. Likewise when the Wesleys and Whitefield studied the Bible together, and attempted to live holy lives, following the example of Christ, they were looked upon as fit subjects for an insane asylum and called "Methodists," or "The Holy Club." The ministers were too often either worldly and fox-hunting, or immoral and licentious, and sometimes led or incited mobs against the Methodists and their adherents. The early Methodists could have made the Apostles words their own: "In journeyings often, in perils of water, in perils of robbers, in perils by countrymen, in perils by the heathen, in perils in the city, in perils in the wilderness, in perils in the sea, in perils among false brethren; in weariness and painfulness, in watchings

often, in hunger and thirst, in fastings often, in cold
and nakedness; besides those things that are without,
that which cometh upon us daily, the care of all the
churches."

While John Wesley was visiting Shepton-Mallet, in
January, 1748, a hired drunken mob pelted him and
his companion, Robert Swindells, with dirt, stones,
and clods and broke the windows of the house in which
they were staying. The mob took it by storm and
further threatened to make it a heap of burning ruins.

Still Methodism spreads as revivals broke out
wherever Methodists wandered. Wesley, writing to
his friend Blackwell on February 2, 1748, says: "Both
in Ireland, and in many parts of England, the work of
our Lord increases daily. At Leeds only, the society,
from a hundred and eighty, is increased to above five
hundred persons."

It should be made clear that the Wesleys and Whitefield were the closest and warmest of friends; but
their courses of action were separate. Whitefield was
a Calvinist in his theology, yet more of a Christian;
the Wesleys were not Calvinists in theology, but
equally as good Christians. Whitefield was an evangelist, John Wesley was an organizer and evangelist, and
Charles Wesley was a musician in the sense of a poet
and hymn writer. Whitefield dedicated his life to the
cause of winning souls to the Christian way of life.
John Wesley dedicated his life no less to the winning
of souls but he also organized them into societies.
Charles Wesley dedicated his life to the task of interpreting life's greatest experience and setting it to music which sent the Methodists into battle against sin
with a song of triumph and praise to God. At every
point of difference between theologies, it can truthfully

be said that the Christian in them dominated. An illustration of the lasting qualities of this bond of Christian fellowship which began in "The Holy Club" at Oxford, is expressed by Charles Wesley when he writes on October 8, 1749, while in company with Whitefield: "The Lord is reviving His work as at the beginning multitudes are daily added to His church. George Whitefield, my brother, and I, are one; a threefold cord, which shall no more be broken. The week before last, I waited on our friend George at our house in New Castle, and gave him full possession of our pulpit and people's hearts, as full as was in my power to give. The Lord united all our hearts."

Who were the Methodists and from whom did they come? Methodists were "twice-born" persons in the New Testament sense. They staked their lives on the fact that Salvation is by faith. Whitefield and the Wesleys began preaching to prisoners, to outcasts in the slums, to the great populace, and likewise to the rich and the nobility, most notable—The Countess of Huntingdon. Of the seventy-eight published letters of Whiltefield, written in 1749, nearly half are addressed to titled ladies.

Horace Walpole in a letter, dated March, 1749, remarks: "Methodism in the Metropolis is more fashionable than anything but brag; the women play very deep at both; as deep, it is much suspected, as the matrons of Rome did at the mysteries of the 'Bona Dea.' If gracious Anne were alive, she would make an admirable defendress of the new faith, and would build fifty more churches for female proselytes."

In another letter dated May 3rd, he wrote: "If you ever think of returning to England, you must prepare yourself with Methodism. This sect increases as fast as almost any religious nonsense ever did. Lady Frances Shirley has chosen this way of bestowing the dregs of her beauty; and Mr. Syttelton is very near making the same sacrifice of the dregs of all those various characters he has won. The Methodists love your big sinners, as proper subjects to work upon; and, indeed, they have a plentiful harvest. Flagrancy was never more in fashion; drinking is at the highest wine mark; and gaming is joined with it so violently, that, at the last New Market meeting, a bank bill was thrown down, and nobody immediately claiming it, they agreed to give it to a man standing by."

George Whitefield wrote: "I am a debtor to all, and intend to be at the head of no party. I believe my particular province is, to go about and preach the gospel to all. My being obliged to keep up a large correspondence in America, and the necessity I am under of going thither myself, entirely prevent my taking care of any societies. I profess to be of a Catholic spirit. I have no party to be at the head of, and, through God's grace, will have none; but, as much as in me lies, strengthen the hands of all, of every denomination, that preaches Jesus Christ in sincerity."

Methodism found root in the social, moral, and spiritual discontent of eighteenth century England. This is expressed in Wesley's description of the origin of the Methodist Societies: "In the latter end of the year 1739, eight or ten persons came to me in London, who appeared to be deeply convinced of sin and earnestly groaning for redemption. They desired (as did two or three more the next day), that I would spend some time with them in prayer, and advise them how to flee from the wrath to come, which they saw continually hanging over their heads. That we might have more time for this great work, I appointed a day when they might all come together, which from thenceforth they did every week, namely, on Thursday in the evening. To these, and as many more as desired to join with them, (for their number increased daily) I gave those advices from time to time which I judged most needful for them; and we always concluded our meeting with prayer suited to their several necessities. This was the rise of the United Society, first in London. and then in other places."

CHAPTER II.

In the midst of this environment, Richard Whatcoat made his first appearance on the 23rd of February, 1736, at the home of Charles and Mary Whatcoat. This was the year that Bishop Benson placed his hands upon the head of George Whitefield in Holy Ordination and gave the sanction of the Anglican Church to the voice and message of the young orator and prophet of the eighteenth century.

The greatest blessing that can come to any lad, is a Christian home. Richard Whatcoat was favored with this blessing. His parents were members of the Established Church. Fortunately, this home received the ministry and pastoral care of a very religious and spiritual man, unique in the clergy of his time. The Rev. Samuel Taylor, the Evangelical and Methodist preacher, preached three times every Sabbath and held weekly class meetings within his own home and at other places in his parish. Wesley writes in the Minutes of the Conference of 1766:

In 1744, I wrote to several clergymen, and to all who then served me as sons in the gospel, desiring them to meet me in London, to give me their advice, concerning the best method of carrying on the work of God. They did not desire this meeting, but I did; knowing that 'in a multitude of counsellors there is safety.' And when their number increased, so that it was neither needful nor convenient to invite them all, for several years I wrote to those with whom I desired to confer, and these only met at the place appointed; till at length I gave a general permission, that all who desired it, might come.

Observe: I myself sent for these, of my own free choice; and I sent for them to advise, not govern me. Neither did I at any of these times divest myself of any part of that power above described, which the providence of God had cast upon me, without any design or choice of mine.

What is that power? It is a power of admitting into, and excluding from, the Societies under my care. Of choosing and removing Stewards, of receiving or not receiving Helpers; of appointing them when, where, and how, to help me; and of desiring any of them to meet me, when I see good. And as it was merely in obedience to the providence of God, and for the good of the people, that I at first accepted this power, which I never sought, nay, a hundred times laboured to throw off; so it is on the same considerations, not for profit, honour, or pleasure, that I use it at this day.

We find the Rev. Samuel Taylor, vicar of Quinton, attending the first Methodist Conference, being held in London, on Monday, June 25, 1744. He was likewise one of the six ministers who constituted the Methodist Conference of 1744. He was in attendance at the conference which met at the New Room in Bristol, May 13, 1746. We have enough evidence here to show that he was more than friendly toward the Methodists; he sanctioned their teachings and became one of them. Therefore, Whatcoat's family was under the influence of the Methodists if in no other way than through the sermons and influence of this minister. It would not be stretching the facts too far, to say that from Whatcoat's statement his mother was an exemplary Methodist in her life and conduct. He, referring to his mother in his memoirs, states: "I believe my mother walked in the form and enjoyed the power of Godliness more than thirty years, and died in the triumph of faith in the year 1771."

His father died while he was very young, leaving his mother a widow with five children—two sons and three daughters. All of the children were trained with the greatest Christian devotion and were brought into the Christian way of life. As his father left but a small estate, the children were deprived of the scant educational opportunities of their day. The educational system of the eighteenth century was not well developed and the poor had a meager chance for an education. His mother, knowing this, realized that it was necessary to teach her boys a trade. Thus, Richard was apprenticed to Joseph Jones of Birmingham. We have no information of the nature or type of trade he acquired. Evidently, it was a good preparation for the work to which he was later called. He was thirteen years old when he began his apprenticeship. He was not long at Birmingham before Jones moved to Darlaston, in Staffordshire, where he served, to the best of his ability, the remainder of his appreticeship

As we piece together the meager facts of these years of his life, we catch a glimpse of his struggles and temptations, and we watch him as he fights through them all to win the crown of strong and vigorous manhood. It was no easy battle to win in the midst of the evil forces prevalent in the eighteenth century. During the eight years of apprenticeship, he tells us, "I was never heard to swear a vain oath, nor was ever given to lying, gambling, drunkenness, or any other presumptuous sin, but was commended for my honesty and sobriety, and from my childhood I had, at times, serious thoughts on death and eternity."

At the expiration of his apprenticeship with Jones, Richard Whatcoat left Darlaston to live in Wednesbury, which was not very far from the scenes of his

old abode. He had just passed the twenty-first mile-
stone of his age when his career opened to him.

The town of Wednesbury was famous for its opportunities of moral decay and opposition to sincere
Christian Religion. To illustrate the conditions prevalent at Wednesbury, we quote from Wesley's Journal
the following:

"I, John Eaton, of Wednesbury, in Staffordshire,
heard the Rev. Mr. Charles Wesley, in the latter end of
the year 1742, preach salvation by faith, in the Coalpit
Field. I and many others rejoiced to hear in particularly, many of the poor people at Darlaston, some of
whom soon after began to meet together in the evenings, to sing, and pray, and read the Bible. Some at
Wednesbury used to go and meet with them; but one
evening the mob at Darlaston rose, pelted them with
clods and stones, and broke all the windows of the
house where they had been.

"On the 30th of May, 1743, John Adams (whose
house it was) fetched a warrant to carry some of the
rioters before Justice P., of Walsal. He desired some
of us of Wednesbury to go with him; so four or five of
us went: but the mob at Walsal immediately rose upon
us; so that we were obliged to take shelter in a public
house. Here we were kept close prisoners till it was
dark, several of us having been much hurt and abused.
When it was night, we escaped one or two at a time.
Francis Ward and I went last.

"On the 21st of June, 1743, a large mob came to my
house at Wednesbury: I was then constable, so I went
to the door with my constable's staff, and began reading the act of parliament against riots; but the stones
flew so thick about my head, that I was forced to leave
off reading and retire; so they broke about half my
windows and went away; but some hours after they
came again and broke all the rest, and the door of my
house, and the clock to pieces. This is a short account
of the first damage that was done to me."

"On the 21st of June, a great multitude gathered together in Wednesbury churchyard: among them was Harvey Walklet of Wednesbury, and Richard Dorset of Darlaston. Harvey said to Richard Dorset, 'Methinks they are not so well armed as I would have them.' Richard answered, 'There are many pretty fellows from Darlaston; I know them to be good blood.' Harvey replied, 'There is John Baker with the oak bough in his hand; he will break the first pane of Mr. Eaton's window.' Accordingly, they went to Mr. Eaton's first, and from thence to other houses. Here are above fourscore houses in and about Wednesbury, in many of which there are not three panes of glass left."

JAMES JONES.

Many of these riots were instigated by the clergy of the Established Church. For example, one was a savage onslaught made upon Methodism by the Rev. John Downs, Rector of St. Michael, Woodstreet, and lecturer of Saint Mary-Le-Bow, London. This was a large pamphlet entitled, "Methodism Examined," being the substance of four discourses from Acts 20:28-30." The following gives a part of these charges:

"The founders of Methodism, in 1734, were too bold, though beardless divines, so young, that they might rather be called wolflings than wolves, novices in divinity, and lifted up with spiritual pride. They were ambitious of being accounted ministers of greater eminence and authority than either bishops or archbishops; missionaries immediately delegated by heaven, to correct the clergy in the true nature of Christianity, and to caution the laity not to venture their souls in any such unhallowed hands as refused to be initiated into all the mysteries of Methodism. Their Journals were ostentatious trash, filled with jargon, that passed for inspiration. Their followers seem to look upon every place upon which they tread, as holy ground; they are comforted and refreshed with their very shadows passing over them; and they follow in crowds, wherever it is noised about, that they are to vociferate.'

"The Methodists deny the necessity of good works; they make their boast, that they are the only persons who know the truth as it is in Jesus Christ, and that all others are unenlightened, and uninformed, interpreting the Scriptures according to the letter which killeth, but ignorant of the Spirit which giveth life. They endeavour to support their weak and wild notions by the abuse and perversion of Scripture, and talk as proudly as the Donatists of their being the only true preachers of gospel truth. They insult the Established Church, despise dominions, speak evil of dignities, and trample all rules and authority beneath their feet. Their doctrines or notions coincide with many of the oldest and rankest heresies, that ever defiled the purity and disturbed the peace of the Christian Church; particularly those of the Simonians, the Gnostics, the Valentinians, the Donatists, the predestinarians, the Montanists, and the antinomians. They treat Christianity as a wild, enthusiastical scheme, which will bear no examination; they will have it, that we may be saved by faith in Christ, without any other requisite on our part; they consider man as a mere machine, unable to do anything towards his own salvation; they represent faith as a supernatural principle, altogether precluding the judgment and understanding, and discerned by internal signs and operations; and they build all their notions upon Scripture authority, putting sacred texts to the torture, and racking them till they speak to their purpose. The whole strength of their cause lies in the perversion of the Scriptures, and the abuse of the clergy. By the most peevish and spiteful invectives, the most rude and rancorous revilings, the most invidious calumnies, they strive to poison the minds of the people against their true and rightful pastors."

The Rev. Downs further characterizes the Methodists as "frightful monsters," as evidenced by the following quotation:

"These new gospel preachers are close friends to the Church of Rome, by harmonizing or agreeing with her in almost everything except the doctrine of merit; they are no less kind to the cause of infidelity, by making the Christian religion a light and airy phantom, which one single breath of the most illiterate freethinker can easily demolish; they cut up Christianity by the roots, by insinuating that a good life is not necessary to justification; they are enemies, not only to the Christian, but to every religion whatsoever, in which reason or common sense hath any share, by labouring to subvert the whole system of morality, and by erecting a proud and enthusiastic faith upon the ruins of practical holiness and virtue."

As a matter of fact, these charges were false, and anyone who desires to substantiate this statement can do so by turning to the Conference Minutes from 1744 to 1749, which deal with the doctrinal bases of Methodism.

In order that we may get the attitude of Mr. Wesley toward these charges made by the clergy of the Established Church, we quote as follows:

If you fall upon people that meddle not with you, without either fear or wit, you may possibly find, that they have a little more to say for themselves than you were aware of. I 'follow peace with all men'; but if a man set upon me without either rhyme or reason, I think it my duty to defend myself, so far as truth and justice permit. Yet still I am (if a poor enthusiast may not be so bold as to style himself your brother),

Reverend sir, your servant for Christ's sake,

JOHN WESLEY.

"Here," says Whatcoat, "I found myself in continual danger of losing the little religion I had, as the family in which I lived had no religion at all." Therefore, he seized upon the first opportunity that came to him to move elsewhere. He states that "a kind Providence directed me to a family that feared God and wrought righteousness."

It was in this latter home that he was brought into closer contact with the Methodists. Immediately, he began attending the Methodist meetings. Here he was brought under the conviction of the Holy Spirit as he listened to the Gospel preached by the Methodists. He relates this experience in the following quotation: "And when the preacher was describing the fall of man, I thought he spoke to me in particular, and spoke as if he had known everything that ever was in my heart. When he described the nature and fruits of faith, I was conscious I had it not, and though I believed all the Scripture to be of God, yet I had not the marks of a Christian believer. And I was convinced that if I died in the state wherein I then was, I should be miserable forever. Yet, I could not conceive how I, that had lived so sober a life, could be the chief of sinners. But this was not long; for I no sooner discovered the spirituality of the law, and the enmity that was in my heart against God, than I could heartily agree to it."

In the language of the poet Cowley, we say

"Happy art thou, whom God does bless
With the full choice of thine own happiness,
And happier yet because thou'rt blest
With wisdom how to choose the best."

CHAPTER III.

Richard Whatcoat had entered in 1757 upon a great and glorious adventure which was to have its discoveries revealed in an altogether unique way. The thing that was about to happen in his own life was what must happen in every life, if life is to have its true significance. If a man is to know other people, he must first know himself. Thus, the first great and potent discovery had come to Richard Whatcoat, when he began to discover himself through an experience of his own. The fascinating thing about all of our experiences is that our minds are not just blank pages upon which our experiences are stamped. Our minds are in the form of new experiences, new ideas, and new relationships made possible by groups of memories which enable us to interpret and to link the old with the new.

All of this is revealed in this marvelous experience of Richard Whatcoat. Instantly, he began to interpret and to analyze his own life, in order that he might have a single excuse upon which he could base his rejection, but none could be found. All the searchlights of God's grace and love were turned upon his soul. The revelation of God's will was gripping his whole being. Listen to his testimony, "The thoughts of death and judgment now struck me with terrible fear. I had a keen apprehension of the wrath of God, and of the fiery indignation due to sinners; so that I could have wished myself to be annihilated, or to be the vilest creature, if I could but escape judgment."

He was in this state of mind when he heard some one say, "I know, God for Christ's sake, has forgiven all my sins. And His Spirit witnesseth with my spirit, that I am a child of God." This gave him new encouragement, and he determined never to rest until he had the witness of the Spirit within himself that his sins were forgiven. There was no rest for him day or night. "Now," said he, "all my virtues, which I had some reliance on once, appeared as filthy rags." At this point many discouraging thoughts came into his mind as he tells us, "many are called but few chosen." "Hath not the potter power over his own clay, to make one vessel to honour and another to dishonour?" From these he interpreted that he "was made to dishonour, and so must inevitably perish." In the words of Shakespeare we say,—

"Poor soul, the centre of my sinful earth,
    Fooled by those rebel powers that thee array,
Why dost thou pine within, and suffer dearth,
    Painting thy outward walls so costly gay?
Why so large cost, having so short a lease,
    Dost thou upon thy fading mansion spend?
Shall worms, inheritors of thine excess,
    Eat up thy charge? Is this thy body's end?
Then, soul, live thou upon thy body's loss,
    And let that pine to aggravate thy store;
Buy terms divine in selling hours of dross;
    Within be fed, without be rich no more:
So shalt thou feed on death, that feeds on men,
    And, death once dead, there's no more dying
        then."

It is very interesting to note the grip which theological concepts of the time had upon the life and thought of young Whatcoat. One could almost recompose the entire system of theology in vogue during the eighteenth century by the study of the spiritual struggles of this young man of twenty-one years. Here we see, in Whatcoat's explanation of his experience, the Anglo-Catholic with a large mixture of Calvinism and Methodism, Methodism predominating. He tells in no unexacting terms, the story of his struggle with God. It rings with certainty and honesty of heart and soul. This was a dark and stirring struggle, burdened, no doubt, with the cumbersome load of medieval theology; nevertheless it was one that neither knows nor admits defeat. Twentieth century religious life needs to rediscover a lost element that was manifest in these men of yesterday. History will testify to the fact that those men whose names are written in the archives of religious leadership are men who have had a great and stirring religious experience. As Cowper has said, in "The Task":

> God gives to every man
> The virtues, temper, understanding, taste
> That lifts him into life, and lets him fall
> Just in the niche he was ordain'd to fill.
> To me an unambitious mind, content
> In the low vale of life.

Richard Whatcoat was now meeting destiny where the great souls of all ages have always met it—alone, in spiritual struggle. It was on September 3rd, 1758, that the great discovery was completed; fear turned to faith, and guilt led to freedom. As he was reading the Scriptures it was as if some one whispered to him. "Thou had'st better read no more, for the more thou readest the more thou wilt know. 'And he that knoweth his Lord's will, and doeth it not shall be beaten with many stripes.'" He paused here awhile and then decided, "Let the consequence be what it may, I will proceed."

"When," he said, "I came to those words, 'the Spirit
itself beareth witness with our spirit, that we are the
children of God,' as I fixed my eyes upon them, in a
moment my darkness was removed, and the Spirit did
bear witness with my spirit, that I was a child of God.
In the same instant I was filled with unspeakable peace
and joy in believing, and all fear of death, judgment,
and hell suddenly vanished away. Before this, I was
kept awake by anguish and fear, so that I could not get
an hour's sound sleep in a night. Now I wanted not to
sleep, being abundantly refreshed by contemplating the
rich display of God's mercy, in adopting so unworthy
a creature as I was to be an heir of the Kingdom of
Heaven."

There must be a battle before there can be a victory. The result of this battle was peace and joy. All
the happiness and pleasure in life which others had
sought by sinning, he sought and found by refusing to
sin. All through the long and weary ages, men sold
their character at the command of the body. Richard
Whatcoat was not to obey the command of the body,
but was to fight through until he had the final assur-
ance. Many might say there was no need to go further
into the struggles and that the final victory for all time
was won. But was it? He was now to hear the hiss
of the serpent with greater self-consciousness than before. Because he had emptied himself of all his sins,
there was a new opportunity for the "invading evil"
to flood his life in a thousand ways. The problem is
not half so easy when we stop to analyze our own lives.
We find that one of the deepest sources of unhappiness
and discontent is found in our own incapacity to har-
monize the forces of our own inner life. Victor Hugo
wrote: "I feel two natures struggling within me."

There seems to be a whole legion of natures all the while contending within us and these natures did not escape Richard Whatcoat. Our lives represent a marvelous collection of unclassified attitudes. They represent a mighty assembly of undisciplined and unmastered forces. All of us would like to come to feel secure and the "captain of our souls." That is just what we are unable to do. We cannot unify the forces of our own life and mould them into harmonious expression. Then from this analysis we look at the practical functioning of the personality of Jesus as He works His way through the Gospels into a deep and vital experience of God in the life of Richard Whatcoat.

In Whatcoat's own narrative he tells us of those natures and conflicts in the following words: "This joy and peace continued about three weeks, after which it was suggested to me, 'Hast not thou deceived thyself? Is it not presumption, to think thou art a child of God? But if thou art, thou wilt soon fall away; thou wilt not endure to the end.' This threw me into great heaviness; but it did not continue long, and to reading and hearing the word of God at all opportunities, my evidence became clearer and clearer, my faith and love stronger and stronger, and I found the accomplishment of that promise, 'They that wait upon the Lord shall renew their strength.'"

This story reveals to us a real soul struggle through the darkest hour just before the dawn of a new day. "Yet," says Whatcoat, "I soon found, that though I was justified freely, yet I was not wholly sanctified. This brought me into a deep concern, and confirmed my resolution, to admit of no peace, no, nor truce, with the evils which I still found in my heart. I was sensible both that they hindered me at present in all my holy exercises, and that I could not enter into the joy of my Lord, unless they were all rooted out. These considerations led me to consider more attentively the exceeding great and precious promises whereby we may escape all the corruption that is in the world, and be made partakers of the Divine nature. I was much confirmed in my hope of their accomplishment, by frequently hearing Mr. Mather speak upon the subject. I saw it was the mere gift of God; and, consequently, to be received by faith. And after many sharp and painful conflicts, and many gracious visitations, on March 28th, 1761, my spirit was drawn out and engaged in wrestling with God for about two hours, in a manner I never did before. Suddenly I was stripped of all but love. I was all love and prayer, and praise, and in this happy state, rejoicing evermore, and in everything giving thanks, I continued for some years; wanting nothing for soul or body, more than I received from day to day."

Here we see influencing his life the doctrines of "Grace and sanctification" preached and taught by the Methodists. This "Mr. Mather," whose first name was Alexander, was one of John Wesley's assistants. John Wesley considered that all of the societies were a united body of which he was the Pastor, and he appointed certain ministers as his assistants and others as local or traveling helpers to his assistants. Therefore, Whatcoat was very definitely guided in his religious experience by Alexander Mather, who, no doubt, was appointed over the circuit where Whatcoat attended his preaching at that time. Thus, we observe his spiritual struggle and conversion.

It is self-evident that a man having such a deep spiritual experience as this could not long keep it to himself. He was bound to share this wonderful blessing with others. Richard Whatcoat, having many rich and wonderful talents with abundant grace, and a heart filled with unfathomable love, began telling others about his religious experience. Soon he became the class-leader for the Methodist Society at Wednesbury, later band-leader and steward of the society. He says, "I began to look around, and to observe, more than ever, the whole world full of sin and misery. I felt a strong desire for others to partake of the same happiness with myself. I longed to declare unto them what I knew of our Saviour. But I first sat down to count the cost; and being then fully convinced of my duty, I began to exhort those of the neighbouring towns to repent and believe the Gospel. This I did for about a year and a half; but was still convinced I might be more useful as a travelling preacher. This I mentioned to Mr. Pawson, a little before the conference in 1769."

John Pawson was then stationed on the Staffordshire Circuit, being an assistant, and at the same time, as associate with John Wesley and John Allen on that circuit. We do not know whether Whatcoat at this time knew John Wesley or not, but evidently John Pawson was well acquainted with Whatcoat and knew likewise, the fine Christian qualities of this young man. Pawson was very glad to recommend him to Wesley and also, no doubt, Whatcoat knew that John Pawson's influence and recommendation would be accepted by John Wesley. At the British Conference in 1769, John Pawson presented his name as a suitable person for the ministry.

Francis Asbury had been received by the Conference two years previous, when it met at London on

August 16, 1767. This fact is interesting because these two names should forever become synonymous with the beginning and formation of the Methodist Episcopal Church in America. Francis Asbury was appointed to the Bedfordshire Circuit, a circuit to which Whatcoat was later sent.

The conference at Leeds opened on Tuesday, August 1, 1769, and we have the following account taken from John Wesley's Journal when he says: "A more loving one we never had. On Thursday I mentioned the case of our brethren at New York, who had built the first Methodist preaching house in America, and are in great want of money, but much more of preachers. Two of our preachers, Richard Boardman and Joseph Pillmoor, willingly offered themselves for the service; by whom we determined to send them fifty pounds as a token of our brotherly love."

This work was growing so rapidly that they requested more missionaries. John Wesley refers to this during the conference which met in Leeds in 1769. Likewise, on December 26th of the same year Wesley says, "I read the letters from our preachers in America, informing us that God had begun a glorious work there; that both in New York and Philadelphia multitudes flocked to hear, and behave with the deepest seriousness; and that the society in each place already contains about 100 members."

John Wesley was referring to the people, who nine years previous, sailed from Ireland, in Limerick County, for New York, on the ship "Perry." The New York "Mercury" for August 18th, 1760, recorded the safe arrival of the Perry after a nine-weeks' voyage from Ireland. These were all members of the Methodist Society in Ballingrane, Ireland. Among them were

Philip Embury, who was a local preacher in the Methodist Society, and Paul Heck and his wife Barbara, who played an important role in the founding of Methodism in America. After a period of about five years, at the request of Barbara Heck, Philip Embury began to preach in his own home in New York. In 1768, the John-Street Methodist Church was erected.

The conference at Leeds likewise, accepted Richard Whatcoat and gave him his first appointment of which he speaks, "He wrote (Mr. Pawson) and let me know, that he had proposed me at the conference, and that I was accepted as a probationer, and stationed in the Oxfordshire circuit." Having settled his temporal affairs with all speed, he entered upon his great mission as a proclaimer of "good news" to all the world and in a special way to those of Oxfordshire circuit. He was an associate of Benjamin Rhodes on this circuit.

CHAPTER IV.

MINISTRY BEFORE THE AMERICAN REVOLUTION.

Richard Whatcoat was thirty-three years old when he took up his work on the Oxfordshire circuit. On October 16, John Wesley visited Oxfordshire, as he states in his Journal, "On October 16, I began my journey into Oxfordshire, and in the evening preached at Henley. A great part of the congregation was perfectly void, both of sense and modesty, but at this time they were unusually quiet, as I did not take them out of their depth in opening and applying those words, 'It is appointed unto men once to die.' "

This statement of Wesley's reveals the character and type of people to whom Whatcoat had been sent to serve as his first pastorate. The membership increased that year by 40. Likewise, it was this conference which passed the resolution that the circuits were to supply the ministers with horses, saddles, and bridles whenever needed.

Also, this Conference passed another resolution which was to authorize the Conference to provide for the ministers' wives, by apportioning a certain amount to the various circuits which were financially able to give such support.

Before the Conference adjourned Wesley read the following paper for the good of the societies.

My dear Brethren—

1. It has long been my desire, that all those ministers of our Church, who believe and preach salvation by faith, might cordially agree between themselves, and not hinder but help one another. After occasionally pressing this in private conversation, wherever I had opportunity, I wrote down my thoughts upon the head, and sent them to each in a letter. Out of fifty

or sixty to whom I wrote, only three vouchsafed me an answer. So I give this up. I can do no more. They are a rope of sand, and such they will continue.

2. But it is otherwise with the "Travelling Preachers" in our connection. You are at present one body: you act in concert with each other, and by united counsels. And now is the time to consider, what can be done, in order to continue this union. Indeed, as long as I live, there will be no great difficulty: I am, under God, a centre of union to all our Travelling, as well as Local Preachers.

They all know me and my communication. They all love me for my works' sake; and, therefore, were it only out of regard to me, they will continue connected with each other. But by what means may this connection be preserved, when God removes me from you?

3. I take it for granted, it cannot be preserved, by any means, between those who have not a single eye. Those who aim at anything but the glory of God, and the salvation of men; who desire, or seek any earthly thing, whether honour, profit, or ease, will not, cannot continue in the connection; it will not answer their design. Some of them, perhaps a fourth of the whole number, will procure preferment in the Church. Others will turn independents, and get separate congregations, like John Edwards and Charles Skelton. Lay your accounts with this, and be not surprised if some, you do not suspect, be of this number.

4. But what method can be taken, to preserve a firm union between those who choose to remain together?

Perhaps you might take some such steps as these:

On notice of my death, let all the preachers in England and Ireland repair to London within six weeks:

Let them seek God by solemn fasting and prayer:

Let them draw up articles of agreement, to be signed by those who choose to act in concert:

Let those be dismissed who do not choose it, in the most friendly manner possible:

Let them choose, by vótes, a Committee of three,

five or seven, each of whom is to be Moderator in his turn:

Let the Committee do what I do now: propose Preachers to be tried, admitted, or excluded. Fix the place of each preacher for the ensuing year, and the time of the next Conference.

5. Can anything be done now, in order to lay a foundation for this future union? Would it not be well, for any that are willing, to sign some articles of agreement before God calls me hence? Suppose something like these:

We, whose names are under-written, being thoroughly convinced of the necessity of a close union between those whom God is pleased to use as instruments in this glorious work, in order to preserve this union between ourselves, are resolved,

I. To devote ourselves entirely to God; denying ourselves, taking up our cross daily, steadily aiming at one thing, to save our own souls, and them that hear us.

II. To preach the old Methodist doctrines, and no other, contained in the Minutes of the Conferences.

III. To observe and enforce the whole Methodist discipline, laid down in the said minutes.

The preachers then requested Wesley to send an extract of this paper to every assistant, in order that the assistant might communicate it to every preacher on his circuit.

Whatcoat served Oxfordshire circuit until Christmas of the same year, when he was sent to Bedford circuit, where he remained until the conference in 1771, which met at Bristol.

The Conference met at London on August 7, 1770, and admitted Richard Whatcoat into full membership of the conference. The following action was taken by this Conference:

A. It is agreed, by all the brethren now met in Conference this 9th day of August, 1770, that no preacher who will not relinquish his trade of buying and selling, or making and vending pills, drops, balsams, or medicines of any kind, shall be considered as a Travelling Preacher any longer. And that it shall be demanded of all those preachers, who have traded in cloth, hardware, pills, drops, balsams, or medicines of any kind, at the next Conference, whether they have entirely left it off or not?

To observe: we do not object to a preacher's having a share in a ship.

Richard Whatcoat was assigned to the Bedfordshire circuit as associate to John Easton and James Perfect. The following advice was given to the preachers by this conference:

Q. 28. What can be done, to revive the work of God, where it is decayed?

A. 1. We must needs visit from house to house, were it only to avoid idleness. I am afraid we are idle still. Do we not loiter away many hours in every week. Try ourselves. Keep a diary of your employment but for a week, and then read it over. No idleness can consist with growth in grace. Nay, without exactness in redeeming time, it is impossible to retain even the life you received in justification. Can we find a better method of visiting, than that set down in the Minutes of 1766, P. 623 c. When will you begin?

Idleness was the terrible sin of the clergy of the Established Church at this time.

The membership on the Bedfordshire circuit increased from 270 to 284, which expresses the material evidence of the spiritual success for this year.

Whatcoat was traveling over the roads which were the scene of John Bunyan's Land which is beautifully described in the following poem by S. J. Stone:

THROUGH BEDFORDSHIRE BY RAIL.

Far behind we leave the clangour of the smoky northern town;

Now we hurry through a country all brown-green and
  sweet grey-brown.
Landscapes gently undulating where light shadows
  softly pass,
Quiet rivers silent flowing through the rarely-trodden
  grass.
Here and there a few sheep grazing 'neath the hedge-
  row poplars tall,
Here and there a brown thatched homestead or a rustic cottage small;
As we rush on road of iron through the fields on
  either hand,
In autumn twilight gravely smiles John Bunyan's land.

More than all the fells and mountains we have passed
  upon our way,
More than e'en that giant city we shall greet ere close
  of day,
Touches us the tender beauty, soft, harmonious, sim-
  ple, quaint,
Of these fields and winding bye-lanes where yet linger,
  sweet and faint,
Echoes of long-vanished ages, rustic homes one might
  have seen
In the old days when John Bunyan played at cat on
  Elstow green,
Meadows still as when he wandered, seeking God;
  while on each hand,
Gravely smiling in the twilight, lay John Bunyan's
  land.

Tender as the closing music of the mighty Dreamer's
  lay,
Lies the country gently round us, all brown-green and
  soft brown-grey.
Tender are our thoughts toward it, as we ponder o'er
  the book
That has travelled through the wide world from this
  homely, rural nook.
Tenderly we name John Bunyan, martyr, poet, hero,
  saint,
Faithful pastor, strong and loving like his Bedford,

simple quaint,
Ah! the happy tears half blind of John Bunyan's land.

John Wesley visited Whatcoat at Bedford, on Friday, October 26, 1770, and said that he preached that day in Bedford while on his journey to London. It was about this time that news came from America, telling of the death of George Whitefield. When Wesley returned to London on Saturday, November 10, he learned of Whitefield's death, and the executors of George Whitefield desired him to preach his funeral sermon on Sunday, November 18th.

"In order to write this," says Wesley, "I retired to Louishome on Monday; and on Sunday following, went to the chapel in Tottenham-Court-Road. An immense multitude was gathered together from all corners of the town. I was at first afraid that a great part of the congregation would not be able to hear; but it pleased God so to strengthen my voice, that even those at the door heard distinctly." Wesley was requested to repeat Whitefield's sermon on many occasions throughout England and Ireland, to which he gladly complied.

Whatcoat served Bedford circuit until the conference at Bristol in 1771. when he was appointed an associate of Robert Wilkinson, James Perfect and John Smith, who served on the Inniskillen circuit, in the northern part of Ireland. This conference sent Francis Asbury and Richard Wright as missionaries to America. The work in America had increased from 669 to 937 in its membership. The American Societies were calling for more missionaries. The call was answered by sending these two splendid young men which increased the number of missionaries to four in America. Francis Asbury writes as follows concerning this conference:

On the 7th of August, 1771, the conference began at Bristol, in England. Before this, I had felt for half a year strong intimations in my mind that I should visit America; which I laid before the Lord, being unwilling to do my own will; or to run before I was sent. During this time my trials were very great, which the Lord, I believe, permitted to prove and try me, in order to prepare me for future usefulness. At the Conference it was proposed that some preachers should go over to the American continent. I spoke my mind, and made an offer of myself. It was accepted by Mr. Wesley and others who judged I had a call. From Bristol I went home to acquaint my parents with my great undertaking, which I opened in as gentle a manner as possible. Though it was grievous to flesh and blood, they consented to let me go. My mother is one of the tenderest parents in the world; but I believe she was blessed in the present instance with Divine assistance, to part with me. I visited most of my friends in Staffordshire, Warwickshire, and Gloucestershire, and felt much life and power among them. Several of our meetings were indeed held in the spirit and life of God. Many of my friends were struck with wonder, when they heard of my going; but none opened their mouths against it, hoping it was of God. Some wished that their situation would allow them to go with me.

I returned to Bristol in the latter end of August, where Richard Wright was waiting for me, to sail in a few days for Philadelphia. When I came to Bristol I had not one penny of money; but the Lord soon opened the hearts of friends, who supplied me with clothes, and ten pounds: thus I found, by experience, that the Lord will provide for those who trust in him.

On Wednesday, September 4, we set sail from a port near Bristol; and having a good wind, soon passed the channel. For three days I was very ill with the sea-sickness; and no sickness I ever knew was equal to it. The captain behaved well to us.

Whatcoat made a hasty call at home to see his mother before leaving, and found she was very ill;

from this illness she never recovered. He spent the night with her, which made her happy. She listened to his story of great adventure which lay before him, and the mission on which he was embarking. No doubt, she realized that this meant the final farewell on this earth; at their next meeting they should greet each other in the world where farewells are unknown. She loved the work to which her son was called; therefore, she gave him up willingly. She lived a few weeks longer before the death angel called for her to come and live that "more abundant life." Whatcoat bade his mother good-bye and set off for his long journey to Ireland. He dreaded the sea voyage. He was an utter stranger to Ireland, of which he had heard many strange and bad reports. This was not a very pleasant period of ministry for him. It took eight weeks to travel through the circuit, preaching and holding meetings two to three times daily, besides visiting the sick, and meeting the societies. The accommodations were very dangerous to health, and there was a scarcity of food. These were trying days to him, and his physical strength was exhausted, but there was much for which to be thankful, for the work prospered and nearly three hundred new members were added to the societies that year.

The conference of 1772 met on August 4th, at Leeds. Richard Whatcoat was appointed to the Armagh circuit as assistant to John Wesley and associated with John William. Wesley comments in the following manner on the proceedings of the conference: "Generally, during the time of conference, as I was talking from morning to night, I had used to desire one of our brethren to preach in the morning. But, having many things to say, I resolved, with God's help, to

preach mornings as well as evenings. And I found no
difference at all: I was no more tired than with my
usual labor; that is, no more than if I had been sit-
ing still in my study, from morning to night."

After conference adjourned, Whatcoat hastened off
to the Armagh circuit. He was taken very seriously ill
on the way to his new appointment. This sickness
lasted for twelve weeks. He was very generously
cared for at the home of the Armstrongs at Sydare.
Then he journeyed on to Armagh circuit where he suffered the return of his sickness, due to venturing too
soon before he had regained his strength. This did not
stop him very long. He soon was traveling and
preaching, when he could hardly sit in the saddle, or
stand up to speak. He did not travel long before he
was stopped for eight more weeks, with his old afflictions. Yet "he endured as seeing him who is invisi-
ble." He was finally restored to better health than he
had enjoyed for many years. We note an increase of
thirty-seven in the membership of the Amagh circuit
this year, while the membership in America had increased to five hundred.

Whatcoat attended the conference in Dublin, in
1773, held by John Wesley, and after its adjournment,
he attended the conference held in London, which met
on August 3rd, of the same year. Wesley says: "I
preached mornings as well as evenings; and it was all
one. I found myself just as strong as if I had preached
but once a day."

Whatcoat was sent by the conference to serve Pem-
brokeshire circuit in Wales having John Boon as his
associate. "This was," says Whatcoat, "an easy,
agreeable, and profitable station to me, and I trust to
the people also; for Mr. Charles Boon and I spent this

year very agreeably among a few loving people." We
see that this was a very enjoyable work and likewise
very successful.

There were now eight missionaries in America and
the membership had increased to one thousand.

At the conference in Bristol, August 8, 1774, What-
coat was assigned to Brecknock, or more correctly,
Brecon circuit, in Wales. Here, associated with Stephen
Proctor and John Broadbent, he ministered for two
years to a faithful people. We find that Brecon is the
birthplace of Thomas Coke. We have no record of
Whatcoat ever meeting Coke while stationed at Brecon.
No doubt Whatcoat knew of the Coke family because
Thomas Coke's father was a prominent citizen of
Brecon, who held several public positions and was very
influential in the religious life of his community.

Wesley visited Brecon circuit on Wednesday, August 24th, of the same year. He comments on this as
follows: "In the evening I preached in the Town Hall
to most of the Gentry in the town. They behaved well,
though I used great plainness of speech in describing
the narrow way."

On the following day Wesley says,

"At eleven I preached within the walls of the old
church at the Hay. Here and everywhere I heard the
same account of the proceedings at ————. The
Jumpers (all who were there informed me) were first
in the court, and afterward in the house. Some of
them leaped up many times, men and women, several
feet from the ground; they clapped their hands with
the utmost violence; they shook their heads; they dis-
torted all their features; they threw their arms and
legs to and fro in all variety of postures; they sung,
roared, shouted, screamed with all their might, to the
no small terror of those that were near them. One

gentlewoman told me, she had not been herself since, and did not know when she should. Meantime the person of the house was delighted above measure, and said, 'Now the power of God is come indeed.' "

Joseph Pillmoor returned this year from America. Things were breaking against the American missionaries because of their English connection. War was in the air. All who had any loyalist leanings were suspicioned and the result was that all the missionaries returned one by one until there were only Francis Asbury and Edward Droomgoole left in America. This year, in the midst of this confused state of affairs, Methodism more than doubled its membership in the American colonies.

The conference at Leeds on August 1, 1775, returned Whatcoat to the Brecon circuit. This was a somewhat stormy session because of certain charges which had been made against certain of the Methodist preachers, as to their proper qualifications. These charges were given a proper hearing before the conference. Wesley states in his Journal:

Having received several letters, intimating that many of the preachers were utterly unqualified for the work, having neither grace nor gifts sufficient for it, I determined to examine this weighty charge with all possible exactness. In order to do this, I read those letters to all the conference; and begged that every one would freely propose and enforce whatever objection he had to any one. The objections proposed were considered at large; in two or three difficult cases, committees were appointed for that purpose. In consequence of this, we were all fully convinced that the charge advanced was without foundation; that God has really sent those labourers into his vineyard, and has qualified them for the work; and we were all more closely united together than we have been for many years.

At this time occurrences which seemed to possess elements of great danger were happening on both sides of the Atlantic. Wesley comments upon the conditions when he says: "Saturday, November 11, I made some additions to the calm address to our American Colonies; need anyone ask from what motive this was written? Let him look round: England is in a flame; a flame of malice and rage against the king, and almost all that are in authority under him. I labour to put out this flame. Ought not every true patriot to do the same? If hireling writers on either side, judge of me by themselves, that I cannot help."

Nearly another thousand were added to the membership of the American church this year and another missionary returned to England.

Wesley again called his preachers to the annual conference which met in London on Tuesday, August 6, 1776. The conference came to a close on Friday, "which we observed with fasting and prayer," says Wesley, "as well for our own Nation as for our brethren in America. In several conferences, we have had great love and unity; but in this there was, over and above, such a general seriousness and solemnity of spirit as we scarcely have had before."

Whatcoat was appointed to Launceston circuit, in West Cornwall. The lines of William Cullen Bryant are appropriate to describe the scenes of West Cornwall.

> The groves were God's first temples, Ere man
>   learned
> To hew the shaft, and lay the architrave,
> And spread the roof above them ere he framed
> The lofty vault, to gather and roll back
> The sound of anthems; in the darkling wood,

Amid the cool and silence, he knelt down,
And offered to the Mightiest solemn thanks
And supplication.

Thomas Hanson, J. Poole and James Skinner were his associates on this circuit. This was, by far, the best appointment he had received to date. The congregations and societies here were large and wide-awake. The total number of members was 1390 for the circuit.

At this point, we note that the situation has grown more tense—even to the breaking point in America. The colonies have, less than a month previous, declared their Independence from their Motherland.

A movement to stop the progress of Calvinism was launched under the following points at this conference.

1. Let all preachers carefully read our tracts, and Mr. Fletcher's and Mr. Sellon's.

2. Let them preach Universal Redemption frequently and explicitly, but in love and gentleness, taking care never to return railing for railing. Let the Calvinists have all this to themselves.

3. Do not imitate them in screaming, allegorizing, calling themselves ordained, boasting of their learning, college, or "My lady." Mildly expose these things, when time serves.

4. Visit as diligently as they do, and insist on Universal Redemption, to everyone newly convinced or converted.

5. Answer all their objections both in public and private, with sweetness both of look and service.

6. Strongly advise our people, not to hear them.

7. Pray constantly and earnestly that God would stop the plague.

Another missionary returned to England from the American colonies.

The voices of Burke, Fox, and Gladstone had been

heard in the halls of Parliament, proposing a variety of ways of reconciliation with the English colonies in America. Reconciliation with the American colonies was thought by many the proper step to be taken by the English Parliament. Likewise, the voice of Patrick Henry was heard to utter the words which became the battle cry of the Revolution, "Give me liberty, or give me death." The spirit of these speeches seemed to express the feeling of a few on both sides of the Atlantic, while England would not heed their noble advice.

It is a remarkable coincidence that Wesley should, so soon after the adjournment of the conference at London, make the acquaintance of Thomas Coke, who should play such an important part in the spreading and organizing of Methodism throughout many lands. Coke was born and educated at Brecon. Thomas Coke was now twenty-nine years of age. He had taken his degrees at Oxford, had been ordained in the Established Church, and was serving as Curate at South Petherton. It was through the influence of the Rev. Brown, at Taunton, that Coke was brought under the influence of Wesley. The Rev. Brown lent to Coke the sermons and Journals of John Wesley, which he read with great delight. On August 13, 1776, Wesley was Brown's guest at Kensington, which made it possible for Coke to meet Wesley.

Wesley writes in his Journal for this date as follows: "I preached at Taunton, and afterward went with Mr. Brown to Kensington. The large, old parsonage house is pleasantly situated close to the church yard, just fit for a contemplative man. Here, I found a clergyman, Dr. Coke, late Gentleman Commoner of Jesus College in Oxford, who came twenty miles on purpose. I had much conversation with him; and a union then began which I trust shall never end."

Coke expressed his doubts respecting his desire of confining himself to one parish. Wesley gripped Coke's hand, and in a manner peculiar to his own said: "Brother, go out and preach the gospel to all the world." Coke returned to his parish meditating upon this greater challenge for service which had come to him that day. From this point we notice something had happened in the life and preaching of Coke. His messages were Methodistic in form and arrangement, as well as in spirit. This was not received very well by the people of his parish, and soon brought about his dismissal by the rector in charge when he abruptly announced at the close of a service that Coke was dismissed. The next time we hear of Coke he is in company with Wesley after the adjournment of the conference which met in Bristol. This note we take from Wesley's Journal.

I went forward to Taunton, with Dr. Coke, who being dismissed from his curacy, has bid adieu to his honourable name, and determined to cast his lot with us.

Henceforth, Thomas Coke was a Methodist preacher, and he was given the task as the great organizer of Methodist missions in other lands.

CHAPTER V.

The conference met at Bristol on August 5, 1777. It was at this conference that Whatcoat was transferred from Launceston circuit in West Cornwall, to St. Austele circuit, in East Cornwall. He had as his associates here, Henry Robbins, Isaac Shearing and James Rogers. There were 718 members on this circuit. "Here," said he, "my faith and patience were strongly exercised; for I felt so sensible for some disorderly members at Plymouth Rock, that my poor heart was almost broke; but I called upon the Lord and he proportioned strength accordingly to my day."

Wesley has the following comment on the character of this conference:

Tues. 5.—Our yearly conference began. I now particularly inquired (as that report had been spread far and wide) of every assistant. Have you reason to believe, from your own observation, that the Methodists are a fallen people? Is there a decay or an increase in the work of God where you have been? Are the societies in general more dead, or more alive to God, than they were some years ago? The almost universal answer was, If we must 'know them by their fruits,' there is no decay in the work of God, among the people in general. The societies are not dead to God: they are as much alive as they have been for many years. And we look on this report as a mere device of Satan, to make our hands hang down.

But how can this question be decided? You, and you, can judge no further than you see. You cannot judge of one part by another; of the people of London, suppose, by those of Bristol. And none but myself has an opportunity of seeing them throughout the three kingdoms.

But to come to a short issue. In most places, the Methodists are still a poor, despised people, labouring under reproach, and many inconveniences; therefore, wherever the power of God is not, they decrease. By this, then, you may form a sure judgment. Do the Methodists in general decrease in number? Then they decrease in grace, they are a fallen, or, at least, a falling people. But they do not decrease in number; they continually increase, therefore, they are not a fallen people. The conference concluded on Friday, as it began, in much love. But there was one jarring string: John Hilton told us, he must withdraw from our connection, because he saw the Methodists were a fallen people. Some would have reasoned with him, but it was lost labour; so we let him go in peace.

The next year found Whatcoat, William Barker and James Perfect at work on the Salisbury circuit, in South Wiltshire, to which they were sent by the Leeds conference, August 4, 1778. This conference was attended by the largest number of Methodist preachers that had ever attended any conference before. Wesley preached morning and evening at the conference. Thomas Coke received his first Methodist appointment to London and Thomas Vasey was admitted into full membership at this conference. Some very good advice is given by the conference on the health of the preacher, which reads as follows:

Q. 23. Why do so many of our preachers fall into nervous disorders?
A. Because they do not sufficiently observe Dr. Cadogan's rules;—To avoid Indolence and Intemperance.
They do indeed use exercise. But many of them do not use enough; not near so much as they did before they were preachers. And sometimes they sit still a whole day. This can never consist with health. They are not intemperate in the vulgar sense; they are

neither drunkards nor gluttons. But they take more food than nature requires; particularly in the evening.

Q. 24. What advice would you give to those that are nervous?

A. Advice is made for them that will take it. But who are they? One in ten, or twenty?

Then I advise:—

1. Touch no dram, tea, tobacco, or snuff.
2. Eat very light, if any, supper.
3. Breakfast on nettle or orange-peel tea.
4. Lie down before ten;—Rise before six.
5. Every day use as much exercise as you can bear:—or
6. Murder yourself by inches.

Parts of this would be good advice for Methodist preachers today, but who wants to take advice? In this respect, have we changed?

The conference adjourned, and the preachers again set off for their fields of labor. Salisbury circuit occasioned the scene to change for Whatcoat, to one of agreeableness and happiness. He describes this experience in the few words, "We had some old faithful members; who were ornaments to their Christian profession, here I laboured two years."

The conference of 1779 opened its session on August 3rd, in London, and it was ascertained that nineteen circuits besides London had lost in membership. Wesley asked, "How can we account for this?"

The following reasons were assigned:

1. Partly the neglect of outdoor preaching, and of trying new places. 2. Partly prejudice against the King, and speaking evil of dignities. 3. But chiefly the increase of worldly mindedness, and conformity to the world. It was also resolved, that no one speaking evil of those in authority, or prophesying evil to the nation, should be a Methodist preacher. Itinerants

were reproved for hastening home to their wives after preaching, and were told, they ought never to do this till they had met the society. To revive the work in Scotland, the preachers were directed to preach in the open air as much as possible; to try every town and village; and to visit every member of society at home.

At the close of this conference, Whatcoat returned to the Salisbury circuit to continue his work there. His associates were transferred and he had David Evans, John Wittam and Richard Seeds as his co-laborers.

Whatcoat attended the conference held in Bristol, on August 1, 1780, and received Northampton circuit as his new field of labour along with Thomas Mitchell. At this conference, it was resolved, "For the future we allow nine or ten days for each conference; that everything, relative to the carrying on of the work of God, may be materially considered." Wesley further states, "I preached on a convenient piece of ground at one end of Radcliff Parade." A great part of the immense congregation had never heard this kind of preaching before; yet they were deeply attentive, while I opened and applied those awful words, 'I saw the dead, small and great, stand before God.'" He further states, "We had the largest number of communicants that had ever met at the New Room; and the largest congregation, at five, than had ever met near King's Square. Wednesday 9—we concluded the conference in much peace and love."

Wesley makes a brief note of the fact that on December 23rd, he visited the societies on the Northampton circuit, to which Whatcoat had been appointed. On the Northampton circuit, Whatcoat was brought in contact with some of his old acquaintances who had counseled him how to gain the heavenly portals. He had been absent ten years from these familiar fields, and he felt very much exalted to find that the work had spread so extensively in such a short time.

When the conference met on August 7, 1781, at Leeds, Wesley remarks in his Journal, "I desired Mr. Fletcher, Dr. Coke, and four more of our brethren, to meet every evening, that we might consult together on any difficulty that occurred. On Tuesday our conference began, at which were present about seventy preachers, whom I had severally invited to come and assist me with advice in carrying on the work of God. Wednesday 8, I desired Mr. Fletcher to preach. I do not wonder he should be so popular; not only because he preaches with all his mind, but because the power of God attends both his preaching and prayer. On Monday and Tuesday we finished the remaining business of the conference and ended it with solemn prayer and thanksgiving."

Wesley makes his visit with Whatcoat on December 10th, at Canterbury circuit where he preached in the evening on the subject, "Casting all your care upon him." Wesley says of this occasion, "It was a word in season." The next day he makes this assertion in his Journal, "Finding abundance of people troubled, as though England were on the brink of destruction, I applied these comfortable words, 'I will not destroy the city for ten's sake.'"

Whatcoat was appointed to Canterbury circuit. There seems to be a little confusion in our accounts of Whatcoat for the years 1780 and 1781. Whatcoat says that he was appointed to Northampton in 1780, but the conference Minutes have him assigned to Kent circuit. Then Whatcoat says that he was sent to Canterbury circuit in 1781, while the Minutes say that he

went to Northampton. Anyway we can forget the
year and place as far as we are concerned. For it was
over these roads, four hundred years earlier, that
Chaucer met those English characters which he made
immortal to the literary world. Whatcoat was upon
another mission to make souls immortal. This was almost accomplished in an instant when a terrible ex-
plosion happened at Featherstone, taking as its toll
three men and many buildings, when Whatcoat in his
Memoirs states, "An awful circumstance happened at
Featherstone: the magazine of gunpowder, of about
seventy barrels, was blown up, and three men blown
to atoms, and the town greatly shaken."

In August, 1782, at the conference in London, Whatcoat associated with J. Ingham, was assigned to Lynn
circuit, in Norfolk county. This conference opened
with a day of fasting and prayer for a blessing on the
ensuing conference. The preachers were greatly
helped and benefited by the spiritual fellowship of
their fellow-ministers. On his arrival in Lynn, Whatcoat sold his horse and travelled the circuit on foot.
He had a very enjoyable pastorate, accompanied with
success in his work.

The conference the following year was held in Bristol, on July 29, 1783. Whatcoat was sent by this conference to the city and circuit of Norwich, in associate
work with Adam Clarke and William Adamson, two
wonderful promising young men in the ministry. This
was a peaceful and fruitful year. Wesley says of this
conference:

Our conference began, at which two points we considered, first; the case of Birstal house; and, secondly,
the state of Kingswood school. With regard to the
former, our brethren earnestly desired that I would go

to Birstal myself, believing this would be the most
effectual way of bringing the trustees to reason. With
regard to the latter, we all agreed, that either the
school should cease, or the rules of it be particularly
observed: particularly, that the children should never
play; and that a master should always be present with
them.

On August 5, Wesley was taken very sick, and the
illness prevented him from further activity until the
latter part of August. Wesley says on the occasion of
his visit to Norwich: "Sunday, October 19, I took the
Diligence for Norwich, and preached there the next
evening, to more than the house would contain; and
both this night and the following, we sensibly felt that
God was in the midst of us."

This conference sent Thomas Coke on a special mission to visit the societies in England to establish the
conference plan in all preaching houses.

It was the closing of fifteen years of active itiner-
ancy in the British Isles, for Whatcoat was now forty-
seven years old, as the scene shifts to a wilderness yet
to be conquered.

In February, 1784, Wesley called Coke into his
study in City Road, London, and spoke to him in substance as follows: As the Revolution in America had
separated the colonies from the mother country forever, and the Episcopal establishment was utterly
abolished, the societies had been represented to him
as in a most deplorable condition; that an appeal had
been made through Mr. Asbury, in which he requested
him to provide some mode of Church government
suited to their exigencies; and that having long and
seriously revolved the subject in his thoughts he had
intended to adopt the plan which he was now about to
unfold; that as he had invariably endeavored in every
step he had taken to keep as closely to the Bible as
possible, so in the present decision he hoped he was not

to deviate from it; that in keeping his eye upon the primitive Churches in the ages of unadulterated Christianity he had much admired the mode of ordaining bishops which the Church of Alexandria had practiced; (to preserve its purity that Church would never suffer the interference of a foreign bishop in any of their ordinations; but the presbyters on the death of a bishop exercised the right of ordaining another from their own body; and this practice continued among them for 200 years, till the days of Dionysius); and finally, that being himself a piesbyter he wished Dr. Coke to accept ordination at his hands, and to proceed in that character to the continent of America to superintend the societies in the United States.

The matter was discussed in the Conference of Leeds and favorably reported. Vasey and Whatcoat were designated by the Conference as men to go with Coke to help with the work. These were ordained elders by Wesley with the assistance of Creighton and Coke—both presbyters of the Church of England—and then Coke was ordained superintendent. Wesley presented them with the following documents which must be read by every one who would understand the origin of American Methodism as a separate Denomination.

I.

To all to whom these presents shall come, John Wesley, late fellow of Lincoln College in Oxford, Presbyter of the Church of England, sendeth greeting.

Whereas many of the people in the southern provinces of North America who desire to continue under my care, and still adhere to the doctrine and discipline of the Church of England, are greatly distressed for want of ministers to administer the sacraments of baptism and the Lord's Supper, according to the usage of the same Church; and whereas there does not appear to be any other way of supplying them with ministers:

Know all men that I, John Wesley, think myself to 'be providentially called at this time to set apart some persons for the work of the ministry in America. And therefore, under the protection of Almighty God, and with a single eye to his glory, I have this day set apart as a superintendent, by the imposition of my hands and prayer (being assisted by other ordained ministers), Thomas Coke, doctor of civil law, a presbyter of the Church of England, and a man whom I judge to be well qualified for that great work. And I do hereby recommend him to whom it may concern, as a fit person to preside over the flock of Christ. In testimony whereof I have hereunto set my hand and seal this second day of September, in the year of our Lord, one thousand seven hundred and eighty-four.

JOHN WESLEY.

As the conference on July 28, 1784, met in session at Leeds, Richard Whatcoat answered to the roll call, but was not concerned about the missionary project to America. "Dr. Coke," says Whatcoat, "and some others offered themselves as missionaries for North America. Although Brother Shadford expressed his desire that I might go, at first it appeared to me as though I was not concerned in the matter; but soon my mind was drawn to meditate on the subject: the power of God came upon me, and my heart was remarkably melted with love to God and man. A prospect of some travels I was likely to go through, if I engaged in that part of the Lord's work, appeared to me—upon which I set apart a day for fasting and prayer."

Before the conference closed, Whatcoat had answered the "Macedonian call" to America, along with Dr. Coke and Thomas Vasey. This meant self-sacrifice and many hardships to be endured by him, "though seeing nothing in the way but the coss, and my own inability for so great a work, I offered myself, if my dear aged father, John Wesley, and my brethren, thought proper."

The following letter will explain itself:

LETTER TO DR. COKE, MR. ASBURY, AND OUR BRETHREN
IN NORTH AMERICA.

Bristol, September 10, 1784.

1.   By a very uncommon train of providences many
of the provinces of North America are totally disjoined
from their mother country, and erected into independent states.   The English government has no authority
over them either civil or ecclesiastical, any more than
over the states of Holland.   A civil authority is exercised over them, partly by the congress, partly by the
provincial assemblies.   But no one either exercises or
claims any ecclesiastical authority at all.   In this peculiar situation some thousands of the inhabitants of
these states desire my advice, and in compliance with
their desire, I have drawn up a little sketch.

2.   Lord King's 'Account of the Primitive Church'
convinced me many years ago, that bishops and presbyters are the same order, and consequently have the
same right to ordain.   For many years I have been
importuned, from time to time, to exercise this right,
by ordaining part of our travelling preachers.   But I
have still refused, not only for peace' sake, but because
I was determined as little as possible to violate the established order of the National Church to which I be-
longed.

3.   But the case is widely different between England and North America.   Here there are bishops who
have a legal jurisdiction: in America there are none,
neither any parish ministers.   So that for some hundred miles together, there is none either to baptize, or
to administer the Lord's Supper.   Here, therefore, my
scruples are at an end; and I conceive myself at full
liberty, as I violate no order, and invade no man's
right, by appointing and sending labourers into the
harvest.

4.   I have accordingly appointed Dr. Coke and Mr.
Francis Asbury to be joint superintendents over our

brethren in North America; as also Richard Whatcoat and Thomas Vasey to act as elders among them, by baptizing and administering the Lord's Supper. And I have prepared a liturgy little differing from that of the Church of England, (I think, the best constituted national Church in the world,) which I advise all the travelling preachers to use, on the Lord's day, in all the congregations, reading the Litany only on Wednesdays and Fridays, and praying extempore on all other days. I also advise the elders to administer the Supper of the Lord on every Lord's day.

5. If any one will point out a more rational and Scriptural way of feeding and guiding those poor sheep in the wilderness, I will gladly embrace it. At present, I cannot see any better method than what I have taken.

6. It has, indeed, been proposed to desire the English bishops, to ordain part of our preachers for America. But to this I object, (1) I desired the bishop of London to ordain only one; but could not prevail. (2) If they consented, we know the slowness of their proceedings; but the matter admits of no delay. (3) If they would ordain them now, they would likewise expect to govern them. And how grievously would this entangle us! (4) As our American brethren are now totally disentangled both from the state, and from the English hierarchy, we dare not entangle them again, either with the one or the other. They are now at full liberty, simply to follow the Scriptures and the primitive church. And we judge it best that they should stand fast in that liberty, wherewith God has so strangely made them free.

"JOHN WESLEY."

The following is a copy of Richard Whatcoat's Certificate of Ordination:

To all to whom these presents shall come, John Wesley, late Fellow of Lincoln College in Oxford, Presbyter of the Church of England, sendeth greeting: Whereas many of the people in the southern provinces of North America, who desire to continue under my care, and still adhere to the doctrines and discipline of the Church of England, are greatly distressed for want of ministers, to administer the Sacraments of Baptism, and the Lord's Supper, according to the usage of the said Church: and whereas there does not appear to be any other way of supplying them with ministers:

Know all men, that I, John Wesley, think myself to be providentially called at this time, to set apart some persons for the work of the ministry in America. And therefore, under the protection of Almighty God, and with a single eye to his glory, I have this day set apart for the said work, as an Elder by imposition of my hands and prayer, (being assisted by two other ordained ministers) Richard Whatcoat, a man whom I judge to be well qualified for that great work. And I do hereby recommend him to all whom it may concern, as a fit person to feed the flock of Christ and to administer Baptism and the Lord's Supper, according to the usage of the Church of England. In testimony whereof, I have hereunto set my hand and seal, this second day of September, in the year of our Lord one thousand seven hundred and eighty-four.

"JOHN WESLEY."

Richard Whatcoat having completed all preliminary arrangements for the trip he left for America on September 28, 1784, at 10:00 A. M., in company with Bishop Coke and Thomas Vasey. They sailed from King's Road, Bristol, en route for New York, in the ship named the "Four Friends" having as its captain John Parrot and, as mate, a man named Phips. The voyage was a very successful one in every way, including sea sickness, for four days they encountered the perils of the stormy sea. Whatcoat said, "the captain and sailors behaved with great civility." They passed the time in study and religious services. The ship was delayed several days by adverse winds which caused them to sail many miles farther than usual.

CHAPTER VI.

THE AMERICAN SCENE.

When Richard Whatcoat arrived in America, he was faced with a new Social Order, because the old order of things under the British Empire had passed. The Revolutionary War had closed; the New Order was in the making. That we may understand American conditions, which Whatcoat was to encounter, we must look back a few years into American history to find the cause for this situation.

If we include in our view, not only the war, but also its immediate causes and consequences, the Revolutionary Period extends from the Stamp Act of 1765, to the close of the century. There are four historic movements, separate, yet continuous, like the four acts of a mighty drama, all having profound influence on the American life, and all crowding into the latter half of the eighteenth century.

The first is social and industrial; it is concerned with the rapid increase in trade and wealth as America's natural resources are discovered, with the spread of education, and with the growth of town as contrasted with country life. For America is no longer an experiment, a "trade venture" as England first regarded her; she is beyond all expectation a success, and has ambition of becoming a nation. Where once the forest stood, dark and silent, the sun now shines on prosperous farmers; the frontier hamlet of log cabins is now a bustling town, and with the town come, inevitably, the newspaper, the high school, the theater, music, poetry, and all fine arts. The church was already established. It came with its first settlers and

was a great influence in producing these later devel-
opments. The church has been, and still is, in many
respects, the foundation stone of social, moral and
spiritual development of community life in America.
Likewise, we cannot ignore the economic influence
upon the Church. We are unable to shake off the elements of the soil, regardless of how hard we try, from
the religious life of the American people.

How very different is this new development from
the Jamestown of John Smith, or the Boston of John
Winthrop.   Here are highways to travel, instead of
the old buffalo and Indian trails. With prosperity and
social pleasures, men begin to think less of theology
and "other worldliness" which were prevalent in the
early days, and more of this present life and its opportunities.

Whittier, who had a keen eye for observation, notes
the changing standards, in "The Preacher," as he looks
upon an old country Church and contrasts it with the
waning glory of Jonathan Edwards:

> Over the roofs of the pioneers
> Gathers the moss of a hundred years;
> On man and his work has passed the change
> Which needs must be in a century's range.
> The land lies open and warm in the sun,
> Anvils clamor and mill-wheels run—
> Flocks on the hillsides, herds on the plain,
> The wilderness gladdened with fruit and grain;
> But the living faith of the settlers old
> A dead profession their children hold;
> To the lust of office and greed of trade
> A stepping-stone is the alter made . . . .
> Everywhere is the grasping hand,
> And eager adding of land to land;
> And earth, which seemed to the fathers meant
> But as a pilgrim's wayside tent;

Solid and steadfast seems to be,
And Time has forgotten Eternity.

SOCIAL AND MORAL CONDITIONS.

Family life of this period, naturally, was at a low ebb. One writer, as to this period, says, "I once cut out of all the newspapers we received the advertisements of all the run-away wives, and pasted them on a slip of paper, close under each other. At the end of a month, the slip reached from the ceiling to the floor of the room. more than ten feet high, and contained more than one hundred and twenty-three advertisements. We did not receive, at most, more than one-twentieth part of the newspapers of the United States."

Dueling was prevalent. It had become a great national sin. Challenges passed within the halls of Congress, and a duelist elected as Vice-President of the United States.

The moral and social safeguards were destroyed—some cities were famous for their disorders, riots, luxury and display. Theaters appeared and laws enacted and re-enacted. for example, in 1784 in Massachusetts, condemning and restricting them. New York and Philadelphia forbid plays and pronounced them immoral. Balls, routs and dancing assemblies, alternating with theaters. were the favorite amusements in Baltimore. It was not until the close of the century that plays were allowed in Boston and elsewhere.

INTEMPERANCE.

The first Continental Congress, in 1774, passed a resolution:

Resolved. That it be recommended to the several legislatures immediately, to pass laws the more effectually to put a stop to the pernicious practice of distilling, by which the most extensive evils are likely to be derived if not quickly prevented.

There was a great increase of this evil, after the Revolutionary War. In 1792, there were 2579 distilleries in the United States.

The first Temperance Association was formed 1789, at Litchfield, Connecticut.

GENERAL CONDITIONS.

"The present time," says Deveraux Jarratt, "is marked by peculiar traits of impiety and such an almost universal inattention to the concerns of religion, that very few will attend, except on Sunday, to hear the word of the Lord. . . . The state of religion is gloomy and distressing, the Church of Christ seems to be sunk very low. . . . Little regard and reverence is paid to Magistrates and persons in public office on account of the prevalence of the Spirit of the French Revolution."

Peter Cartwright says in his Autobiography that, "Logan county, when my father moved into it (1793), was called 'Rogue's Harbor.' Here, many refugees, from almost all parts of the Union, fled to escape punishment or justice; for, although there was law, yet it could not be executed, and it. was a desperate state of society. Murderers, horse-thieves, highway robbers, and counterfeiters fled there, until they combined and actually formed a majority. Those who favored a better state of morals were called 'regulators.' But they encountered fierce opposition from the 'Rogues' and a battle was fought with guns, pistols, dirks, knives, and clubs, in which the 'Regulators' were defeated."

The second great movement, leading toward the

climax of union and nationality, takes us into the midst
of the tumult and upheaval which followed the Stamp
Act of 1765, and the intense agitation over other
measures of taxation, which aroused the colonies in
opposition to England. And perhaps the most note-
worthy thing in this fateful movement is its unex-
pectedness. Only two years earlier the whole country
had rejoiced with England over the treaty of Paris,
which meant two blessings to the colonies: first, the
raids, massacres and general cruelty of the French
and Indian War were all in the past, and second, English rather than French ideals had finally prevailed in America, leaving man free to work out his
own salvation, not in the shadow of military despot-
ism, but in the full sunshine of Anglo-Saxon liberty.
To make such peace, and such opportunity possible,
the colonies had given twenty thousand of their young
men and a sum equal to forty millions of our present
money; and they were content with their sacrifice.

At the very season of their rejoicing, King George
and his ministers resolved, with colossal stupidity, on
two measures: First, that the colonies were to be taxed
by the British Parliament to support a British Army;
and second, that no settlers should be allowed west of
the Allegheny Mountains. That the tax was small was
of no consequence; it was the big injustice that struck
the loyal Colonists like a blow in the face. Just as the
rich Ohio and Mississippi Valleys were cleared of
French troops, our pioneers, pressing eagerly into the
spacious country, must halt and turn back into a narrow land, because an English King had made a covenant with the King of France. They decreed that the
beautiful and splendid territory west of the Allegheny
Mountains should be left forever to the wandering

tribes of Indians. Such decrees were not to be obeyed
by free, democratic spirited men. While towns and
cities of the Atlantic coast were in a stir over one
proclamation, the pioneer of the woods and mountains
quietly ignored the other. Thus loyalty was changed
to distrust, and the Revolution began while Americans
still treasured the memories of a war in which they had
fought shoulder to shoulder with Englishmen against
a common enemy.

The first effect of the Stamp Act, and of the confusion which followed it, was to unite the colonies and
prepare the way for Nationalism. The colonies contained at this time only a million and a half of widely
scattered people. There was no particular grouping
of interests; each colony stood firm by itself, zealously
guarding its own rights. There were superficial differences among them, and doubtless certain colonies
had more frequent and intimate contact with England
than they had with each other. When the first Continental Congress met at Philadelphia, in 1774, our attention is called, not to the divisions and differences
among them, but rather to their unity, their harmony,
their likenesses. Here were fifty-five delegates gathered from the four corners of a vast territory. Here
were Cavaliers, Puritans, Catholics, Protestants, ministers, teachers, merchants, and artisans. All these
men spoke the same language, cherished the same
ideals, and were ready to elect and follow the same
leaders. The words of Otis and Samuel Adams had
been heard far beyond the borders of Massachusetts,
and Patrick Henry's speech had rung like a bugle call
through all the American colonies.

Yet there was no nation on this side of the Atlantic.
There was a prophet whose voice had been heard when

South Carolina said, "The whole country must be ani-
mated with one great soul, and all Americans must
resolve to stand by one another even unto death."
This was the echo of the prophet of the Pilgrims, Governor Bradford, who had voiced the same noble sen-
timent almost a century and a half earlier. Of all the
spoken or written words of the eighteenth century,
these seem to a biographer or historian, the most significant. That "One great soul," all aflame with the
love of freedom and justice, symbolizes the unity of
aim and spirit among the colonies immediately pre-
ceding and during the Revolution.

The third historic movement in the stirring scene
is the Revolutionary War, that scene of struggle
against odds, which makes the blood of an American
tingle anew every time he reads of it. We are so ac-
customed to think of it, and of our independence, as
the result of a supreme effort of the American people,
that it brings surprise to learn that the Revolution
was fought and won by only a part, perhaps the
smaller, and, in respect to this world's goods, probably the poorer part of our colonial ancestors. The
heroism of the war consists partly in this; that the
Continental Army had to fight front and guard the
rear at the same time; that while it faced a superior
force of open enemies, behind it was a larger body of
American Tories, foes of its own household, ready at
any moment to give secret or open aid to the British.
The wedge which split our American life into two
sections was the famous Declaration of Independence,
which is commonly considered the symbol of National
Unity.

As we have noted, the year 1774, when the first
Continental Congress assembled, found the American

colonies singularly united in spirit. Up to that time, and even later, they were loyal to England, and only a few old, visionary spirits, like Henry, and Samuel Adams, had dreamed of a separation from England. At Bunker Hill, Ticonderoga, and Charleston, the colonists were fighting, not for Independence, but expressly for their rights as English subjects.

George Washington wrote on July 3, 1775, "When I first took command of the Continental Army, I abhorred the idea of independence." Then, sudden and startling as a thunderbolt to a great part of the country, came the Declaration of Independence; and every man was called upon to make instant decision between the new and the old. It was a tense, dramatic moment, like that in which Elijah built his altar on Mount Carmel and cried aloud to his people: "How long halt ye between two opinions?" It meant not only separation of nation from nation; it separated a man from his neighbors and friends, and even a father from his own sons and daughters. Our histories are often eloquent —and rightly so—on the subject of Benjamin Franklin's patriotism; but they are silent concerning Franklin's son, who accepted a British office here, probably also a British bribe, and was a Tory, a secret enemy of the cause for which his father labored. There is a fine stirring story of Edmund Randolph, and of many other young patriots, whose hearts ran ever ahead of their Virginia thoroughbreds as they hastened at the first call to join the army of Washington; but we hear little at this time of the father, John Randolph, who followed the English governor, Dinsmore, over seas, and remained a Tory exile during the Revolution. These are but types of thousands of such family divisions.

Thus, the ringing of the famous Liberty Bell, on July 4, 1776, divided the country for the first time into two hostile parties: the Whigs, or Patriots, who supported the new government, and the Tories, or Loyalists, who remained true to old England, as their fathers had been before them. It is essential that we note that there was no separation into North, Middle, and South; but every colony, every town and hamlet, was a house divided against itself. The Whigs were the younger, the mose enthusiastic party, and speedily gained control of the state governments. For them, the bells rang, the cannon roared, the bonfires blazed toward the heavens; but we must not assume that this voiced the joy of a whole nation. For every man who ran out to join the jubilation, there was another man who hurried into his house in grief or rage. Nor are we to conclude, from the Revolutionary literature which survives on our bookshelves, that the young Patriots monopolized the patriotism of the land. The Tories were quite as sincere, quite as patriotic, quite as liberty-loving; only they sought liberty, as all colonists had done for a century past, by maintaining their rights as Englishmen. Utterly misjudging the new movement, they regarded the Patriots as ungrateful rebels; many of them took up arms to suppress the "unholy rebellion." Many more gave secret aid to the British. The Patriots, on the other hand, sadly misjudged their opponents, calling them traitors to the cause of liberty. Thousands of intelligent Loyalists were driven out of the country, and their property confiscated. Thousands more were looked upon with suspicion or hatred. In Loyalist counties, a too-zealous Whig was promptly ostracized, or hanged, as the case might be; in Patriot districts, a suspected Tory might be ridden out of town on a rail, or else given a horrible coat of tar and feathers. Altogether it was a hard and bitter separation of old friends and neighbors, so bitter that in many places the Revolution seemed more like a barbarous civil strife than a united struggle against foreign oppression. Such historical novels as Simms' "The Partisan" and Cooper's "The Spy" give vivid pictures of this civil strife in the Carolinas and portray the plots of Whig and Tory in New York.

The sacrifice of human life was also great, 80,000 Americans perishing, or one for every forty of the inhabitants. Twelve or thirteen cities and numerous villages were burned to ashes. Industry was fatally crippled, and demands were made upon the resources of the country which but few families could afford to sustain. The virtuous sons of many households were transformed into dissipated, discontented, ruined men. Numerous houses of worship were either destroyed or so seriously desecrated and injured as to be of no further service. These were some of the common sufferings of the people.

The fourth great movement of this period is political and includes the long struggle to form a National Constitution. It is the most tense, the most critical, the most fateful movement in all our history. To understand this, we must remember that democracy in America has two essential elements: representation and federation. The first was inherited from England by the Colonists, who, from the beginning, showed their training and independence by electing their own representatives to the House of Burgesses or Assembly or General court, as the Colonial legislatures were variously called. The second element, federation, was new in the world. The problem of welding a number of free states into a single free nation had never been solved, or even attempted; and America, as she set herself to the mighty task, had no precedent to guide her. Alone, and amid endless difficulties, she began her work. Her people were hopelessly divided over questions of state and personal rights involved in or threatened by federation; and the effort to form a Nation came near disrupting the Colonies just after the Revolution had united them. Again there were two parties: the Federalists, who thought first of the Nation and sought as much power as possible for the National Government. The Anti-Federalists, who distrusted and feared the Monarchial tendency of every centralized government since time began, and who were determined to keep the governing power as largely as possible in the hands of the individual states. The struggle reached a climax in Philadelphia in 1787, when Washington called to order the Colonial leaders in thought and in action. "An assembly of demigods," Jefferson called them. After four months' debate they produced the Constitution of the United States, "the noblest work," said Gladstone, the great English statesman, "ever struck off at a given time by the mind and purpose of man."

The defects in the Articles of Confederation became increasingly apparent each year, and the inconveniences which grew out of them, were becoming so serious as to threaten the dissolution of the National Government. The following letter was written by James Madison to Edmund Randolph, dated February 25, 1787, which says:

"Our situation is becoming every day more and more critical. No money comes into the Federal treasury, no respect is paid to the Federal authority, and people of reflection unanimously agree that the existing confederacy is tottering to its foundation. Many individuals of weight, particularly in the Eastern District, are suspected of leaning toward monarchy. Other individuals predict a division of the states into two or more confederacies. It is pretty certain that if some radical amendment of the single one cannot be devised and introduced, one or other of these resolutions, the latter, no doubt, will take place. I hope you are bending your thoughts seriously to the great work of guarding against both."

Somewhere in the midst of all this mighty struggle, our national life began. But as a nation we have no "natal festival" for the simple reason that none can tell us when America was born. Perhaps it was, as Emerson says:

> By the rude bridge that arched the flood,
> Their flag to April's breeze unfurled,
> Here once the embattled farmers stood
> And fired the shot heard round the world.

Possibly it was, as some date it, at the first Continental Congress; or as others say, at the Declaration of Independence. Even others say it was at the inauguration of Washington, whose noble personality held the discordant states together until the new government was established and organized. Even a few choose to follow Lowell, who, with fine poetic insight, places the birth of the Nation on the day when Washington took command of the Army, which was no longer Provincial but Continental, on July 3, 1775. Lowell writes. "Under the Elm."

> Never to see a nation born
> Hath been given a mortal man,

> Unless to those who, on that summer morn,
> Gazed silent when the great Virginian
> Unsheathed the sword whose fatal flash
> Shot union through the incoherent clash
> Of our loose atoms, crystallizing them
> Around a single will's unpliant stem,
> And making purpose of emotion rash.
> Out of that scabbard sprang, as from its womb,
> Nebulous at first but hardening in a star,
> Through mutual share of sunburst and of gloom
> The common faith that made us what we are.

Sketched briefly are the manifold calamities of the Revolutionary War such as the ravaging of the country, the burning of towns, the spirit of fury, vindictiveness and hatred which fired the hearts of multitudes, and all of their influence upon the religious life of the American people. In fact, the war was an event of great religious as well as political significance. It was detrimental to morals and religion.

There was no part of society, public, private, social, secular, or religious, which did not suffer. The country was impoverished and exhausted. The financial cost of the war amounted to $170,000,000.00, a greater expenditure, in proportion to the wealth of the country, than twenty times that sum would be at the present time. A considerable portion of this amount remained in the form of a debt.

The parish ministers in those days commanded unbounded influence and profound respect, and effectively molded thought in civil as well as ecclesiastical matters. The early colonial reverential regard for the clergy had not waned much in New England at the time of the Revolution.

The ministers, like the average population, were separated. Naturally, the Episcopal Church was the

greatest sufferer because of its clergy being almost
wholly foreigners and loyal to the English Crown.
Most of the clergy of the Episcopal Church fled the
country; only a few were friends of the colonies, and
of the cause of liberty. The pulpits of the country
rang with the notes of freedom. The ministers of
other denominations blessed the war and called the patriotic sons of the soil to the support of the American
cause.

The Methodist Church was scarcely ten years old
in America, when national independence was declared,
and it was not organized as the Methodist Episcopal
Church until eight years later; but it was already an
active, earnest and growing power, The first Methodist Missionaries came from England in 1769. Later
under the ecclesiastical direction of John Wesley, public suspicion was provoked against the Methodists.
All but Asbury and Edward Droomgoole returned to
England at the outbreak of or during the Revolution.
Wesley, however, gave much occasion to this suspicion by his "calm address to the American Colonies,"
and many other utterances. This was before the war,
and it is due Wesley to say that when the war really
began, he was on the side of the colonists. This dis-
loyalty was unfounded, but nevertheless, Methodists
suffered and came to be regarded as a dangerous people. The day after the news of the battle of Lexington and Concord came to England, Wesley wrote to
Lord North, the Earl of Dartmouth, saying:

My Lord, whether my writings do any good or no,
it need do no harm; for it rests with your lordship
whether any eye but your own shall see it.

I do not enter upon the question whether the Americans are in the right or in the wrong. Here all my

prejudices are against the Americans for I am a high churchman, the son of a high churchman, bred up, from my childhood, in the highest notions of passive obedience and non-resistance; and yet, in spite of all my long rooted prejudices, I cannot avoid thinking, if I think at all, that an oppressed people asked for nothing more than their legal rights, and that in the most modest and inoffensive manner that the nature of the thing would allow. But waiving all considerations of right and wrong, I ask, is it common sense to use force towards the Americans? These men will not be frightened; and it seems they will not be conquered so easily as was at first imagined.

This letter reveals that Wesley possessed a keen insight into the American situation, but it likewise reveals the great mistake Wesley made which he could never rectify.

In some sections of the country, American born Methodist preachers, such as Waters, Garrettson, Cooper, Hartley, Boyer, Gatch, Abbott and others, in the midst of many embarrassments and stern conflicts, pursued their ministry, zealously exhorting, preaching and building up societies.

In Maryland, where the Methodist preachers were the most numerous, the civil magistrates seemed to be disposed to construe every legal restriction vigorously against them. Some of the preachers were fined, and others were imprisoned, for no other offence than traveling and preaching the Gospel. In the midst of these humiliations and sufferings they toiled and triumphed. Francis Asbury was arrested near Baltimore, and fined, not because he had been guilty of any crime against the new government, but because he, in common with his brethren, was suspected of having loyalist leanings toward the Church of England, and therefore, of entertaining dangerous political views.   He was afterward released and he discontinued preaching, retiring to the home of a friend, Judge White, where he lived for two years probably unknown to the civil authorities.

At the close of the war it was found that the number of Methodist preachers had more than doubled, and the membership had increased two and a half fold. It was the result of an unsurpassed zeal and prudence in the midst of difficulties.   Probably no other religious body can show such a record of progress during this trying period, considering all the other sects which were more favorable toward the cause of liberty, such as Congregational, Baptist, Presbyterian, Quakers and many of the other religious bodies.

The Presbyterian and Baptist Churches were likewise affected by the Revolutionary War.   Rev. E. H. Gillett says of the Presbyterian Church that "The influence of the war upon the condition and prospects of the Presbyterian Church throughout the country was most disastrous.   Its members were almost decided patriots, and its ministers almost to a man, were accounted arch-rebels.   Their well-known views and sympathies made them especially obnoxious to the enemy, and to be known as a Presbyterian was to incur all the odium of a 'Whig.'   It is not strange, therefore, that they should have been the marked victim of hostility, or that they should have been in many cases, mercilessly molested in property and person.   In initiating the Revolution, and in sustaining the patriotic resistance of their countrymen to illegal tyranny, the ministers of the Presbyterian Church bore a conspicuous and even a foremost part. . . .   They preached the duty of resisting tyrants.   They cheered their people in the dreary periods of the conflict by inspiring lofty trust in the God of Nations. Some of them were engaged personally, in the army; some occupied a place in the civil councils; others were personal sufferers from the vengeance of an exasperated foe; and others still sealed their devotion to their country by their blood."

The churches were turned into hospitals, prisons, stables, and riding schools. At the close of the war the country was impoverished and the currency had depreciated. The churches were in a tragic state, religion in confusion, and liberty and freedom were running riot. For many years, the situation seemed hopeless.

There were many new sects springing up or splitting away from the other denominations, either on the grounds of dissatisfaction and unrest, or for slight differences in doctrinal points.

Hildreth, in his History of the United States, says: "The Church of England, the great majority of whose members were Loyalists, lost by the Revolution the establishment it had possessed in the Southern colonies, and the official countenance and the privileges it had enjoyed in New York and New Jersey. But it retained its parsonages, glebe-lands and other endowments, which in some of the States, and especially in the City of New York, were by no means considerable."

Bancroft says, "There were not wanting those who cast a lingering look on the care of the State for public worship. The conservative convention of Maryland declared that 'the Legislature may, in their discretion, lay a general and equal tax for the support of the Christian religion, leaving to each individual the apportioning the money collected from him to the sup-

port of any particular place of public worship or minister;' but the power granted was never exercised. For
a time Massachusetts required of towns or religious societies 'the support of public Protestant teachers of
piety, religion and morality' of their own election;
but as each man chose his own religious society, the
requisition had no effect in large towns, and was
hardly felt elsewhere as a grievance. In Connecticut,
the Puritan worship was still closely interwoven with
the State, and had molded the manners, habits and
faith of the people; but the complete disentanglement
was gradually brought about by inevitable processes
of legislation."

In brief, this was the scene into which Richard
Whatcoat came. On Wednesday, November 3, 1784,
at 11:00 A. M., they arrived at New York. They were
given a warm and kindly reception by the Christian
friends of the society. They remained in New York
until Friday when Coke and Whatcoat left in a stage
coach for Philadelphia. They arrived in Philadelphia,
Saturday evening at 7:00 o'clock. "On the 11th we
borrowed two horses," says Whatcoat, "and rode to
Wilmington, from thence to the Cross Roads, where
Mr. John Coles received us. From thence to Dover,
where Mr. Bassett gave us hearty welcome. We rode to
Murderkill in Kent County. Dr. Coke preached, and
we gave the Sacrament to some hundreds. We held a
love-feast, and a more comfortable time I have not
enjoyed in some years."

They continued their journey on to Barratt's
Chapel where they conducted a meeting. Here they
met Francis Asbury, who says, "I came to Barratt's
Chapel; here, to my great joy, I met those dear men of
God, Dr. Coke and Richard Whatcoat, we were greatly

Interior view of Barratt's Chapel. It was at this altar Asbury, Coke and Whatcoat knelt in consecration for the task of organizing American Methodism. The bench before the altar is the original bench upon which Coke and Asbury sat discussing the plans for the future work of Methodism.

comforted together. The doctor preached on 'Christ our wisdom, righteousness, sanctification, and redemption.' Having had no opportunity of conversing with them before public worship, I was greatly surprised to see Brother Whatcoat assist by taking the cup in the administration of the Sacrament."

After the service, they reveal to Asbury the designs of John Wesley on the steps which he desired to be taken for the future of American Methodism. Asbury says, "I was shocked when first informed of the intention of these my brethren in coming to this country; it may be of God. My answer then was if the preachers unanimously choose me, I shall not act in the capacity I have hitherto done by Mr. Wesley's appointment."

Immediately steps were taken to carry them into execution. It was agreed to call a general conference of the preachers, to be held on Christmas in Baltimore, at which time the organization of the Methodist Societies into an independent Episcopal Church could be fully discussed and carried into effect. This meeting at Barratt's Chapel came to a unique conclusion. After kneel at the altar in prayer, they arose and set out to realize their goal. Freeborn Garrettson was sent into Virginia and the South to call together the ministers for the Christmas conference and all the other ministers who could be reached at that time were notified.

The spot where this event took place is sacred in my memory, for in 1926 while standing on the inserted memorial triangular plate which symbolizes the spot where these great souls consecrated themselves to the tremendous task of American Methodism I was received on probation into the Wilmington Conference. Then on September 15, 1928, I was married to Mary

Catherine Gibson, standing in the same place. Again on October 1, 1933, I was there ordained an Elder to full membership in the Wilmington Conference by Bishop Edwin H. Hughes, having previously been elected at its annual session at Rehoboth, Delaware. For me the words of God were as real as to Moses, "For the ground on which thou standest is Holy Ground." There is none holier or more sacred than Barratt's Chapel. Likewise there were never more holy knees ever bowed before any altar than those that knelt at Barratt's Chapel on November 14, 1784.

Whatcoat returned with Asbury to Dover, where they continued to hold quarterly meetings in the nearby societies. Whatcoat began visiting the societies, en route to Baltimore, where he preached, and met many of his brother ministers. Until the conference convened, the time was faithfully employed in preaching. On December 24, 1784, Asbury, Coke and Whatcoat arrived in Baltimore. Whatcoat says: "We began our conference at 10:00 o'clock, in which we agreed to form a Methodist Episcopal Church, in which the Liturgy (as presented by Rev. John Wesley) should be read, Sacraments to be administered by a Superintendent, Elders, and Deacons, who shall be ordained by a Presbytery, using the Episcopal form, (as prescribed in the Rev. Mr. Wesley's prayer book.)"

"Persons to be ordained are to be nominated by the Superintendent, and elected by conference; and ordained by imposition of the hands of the Superintendent and Elders."

The plan of Wesley met with general approval, Coke and Asbury were elected bishops, to preside over the conference and the general work of the new Church. The rules were formulated and the Methodist Episcopal Church of America came into being. Resolutions were passed to build a college at Abingdon, Maryland, twelve elders and one deacon were ordained, and the conference adjourned on January 2, 1785.

Hon. N. S. Barratt says:

Up to the close of the year 1784, 'the people called Methodists' in this country, as in England, were simply 'societies.' Under the supervision of Mr. Wesley, none of their preachers being permitted to baptize or administer the Lord's Supper, but being required to counsel and direct all the members to follow their example in seeking these sacred ordinances at the hands of ministers who had been ordained by Bishops of the Established Church of England. There is small wonder that some of them, preachers as well as not a few of their people, grew very restive under such irritating restriction; especially after Lowth, Bishop of London, refused Wesley's request to ordain at least two priests who could administer the sacraments to American Methodists, but the affectionate reverence felt for Mr. Wesley and the towering influence of his American representative, the intrepid and self-sacrificing Asbury, had hitherto stayed the rising tide of dissent, with a brief exception of very limited extent. Now, however, the United States had been recognized by Great Britain as an independent nation, and ecclesiastical independence was naturally coincident with civil and political freedom. Wesley did not intend it to be a separate church but a missionary movement within the Church of England, of which he was a member and which he believed to be the best church in the world.

Dr. McConnell sums it up by stating: "But the great spreading branch grew too heavy to be sustained by the slender stem of the American Church, ... and it broke away by its own weight."

Honorable Norris S. Barratt states in a footnote that

Thomas Vasey, two years after his arrival, for some reason accepted reordination at the hands of

Bishop William White of The Protestant Episcopal Church. He soon afterwards returned to London and accepted a curacy. But the old Methodist habit was strong, and he returned to the Wesleyan connection and was stationed at City Road Chapel, where he read the liturgy of the Church of England as Mr. Wesley's will directed. He subsequently lived in Leeds, where he died, December 27, 1826.

CHAPTER VII.

Immediately after the conference ended, Richard Whatcoat commenced his work as an itinerant preacher, in the capacity of the presiding elder over Queen Anne, Talbot and Dorset circuits. His service was visited by marvelous demonstrations of the Spirit. The people were anxious to have the truth, and his time was overcrowded with quarterly meetings and administering the ordinances of the Church. There was a great need for ordained Ministers to aid in this work.

On May 22, 1785, Whatcoat says, "I preached at Wharton, in Kent County in the morning, and baptized 36 children, and in the afternoon I preached at John Angers, and baptized 50 more." This illustrates the great need of ordained Ministers for this work.

At the conference held at Baltimore, June 1, 1785, he was appointed as presiding elder to Baltimore and Frederick circuits. The congregations were small on these circuits for Whatcoat says, "Here we had a few honest and faithful souls."

At this conference Asbury was taken sick and was unable to attend every session. However, he was not detained long by this illness. On Thursday Bishop Coke left on his return voyage to England. Asbury says of this, "We parted with heavy hearts." Evidently Coke had finished the work for which he had come to America. With no further duties, he returned to England in order that he might continue the missionary work in other places. At this time there was much discussion on the subject of separation from the church. We have the following treatise written by Wesley, on August 30, 1785:

1. Ever since I returned from America, it has been warmly affirmed, "You separate from the Church." I would consider how far, and in what sense, this assertion is true.

2. Whether you mean by that term, the building so called, or the congregation, it is plain I do not separate from either; for wherever I am, I go to the church, and join with the congregation.

3. Yet it is true that I have in some respects varied, though not from the doctrines, yet from the discipline, of the Church of England; although not willingly, but by constraint. For instance, above forty years ago, I began preaching in the fields; and that for two reasons, —First, I was not suffered to preach in the churches; Secondly, no parish church in London or Westminster could contain the congregation.

4. About the same time, several persons who were desirous to save their souls, prayed me to meet them apart from the great congregation. These little companies (societies they were called) gradually spread through the three kingdoms. And in many places they built houses in which they met, and wherein I and my brethren preached. For a few young men, one after another desired to serve me, as sons in the Gospel.

5. Some time after, Mr. Deleznot, a clergyman, desired me to officiate at his chapel in Wapping. There I read prayers, and preached and administered the Lord's Supper to a part of the society. The rest communicated either at St. Paul's, or at their several parish churches. Meantime, I endeavoured to watch over all their souls, as one that was to give an account; and to assign to each of my fellow labourers the part wherein I judged he might be most useful.

6. When these were multiplied, I gave them an invitation to meet me together in my house at London; that we might consider in what manner we could most effectually save our own souls, and them that heard us. This we called a conference; meaning thereby, the persons, not the conversation they had. At first I desired all the preachers to meet me; but after-

ward only a select number.

7. Some years after, we were strongly importuned by our brethren in America to go over and help them. Several preachers willingly offered themselves for the service; and several went from time to time. God blessed their labours in an uncommon manner. Many sinners were converted to God; and many societies formed, under the same rules as were observed in England; insomuch, that at present the American societies contain more than eighteen thousand members.

8. But since the late revolution in North America, these have been in great distress. The clergy, having no sustenance, either from England, or from the American states, have been obliged almost universally to leave the country, and seek their food elsewhere. Hence those who had been members of the Church, had none either to administer the Lord's Supper or to baptize their children. They applied to England over and over; but it was to no purpose. Judging this to be a case of real necessity, I took a step which, for peace and quietness, I had refrained from taking for many years; I exercised that power which I am fully persuaded the great Shepherd and Bishop of the Church has given me. I appointed three of our labourers to go and help them, by not only preaching the word of God, but likewise by administering the Lord's Supper and baptizing their children, throughout that vast tract of land, a thousand miles long, and some hundreds broad.

9. These are the steps which, not of choice, but necessity, I have slowly and deliberately taken. If any one is pleased to call this separating from the Church, he may. But the law of England does not call it so; nor can any one properly be said so to do, unless out of conscience he refuses to join in the service, and partake of the sacraments administered therein.

JOHN WESLEY.

On May 7, 1786, at a conference at Abingdon, Md., Whatcoat was assigned as Elder to Kent, Talbot, Dorset and Dover circuits where he labored for three months.   Time and time again we have accounts of great meetings of spiritual awakening wherever he administered the Sacrament of the Lord's Supper.   In September he was sent to preside over the Philadelphia circuit.   Here he spent about eight months. During May, June, and July, 1787, he returned to Baltimore circuit, and then removed to Alleghany, Bath, and Berkley circuits; here he remained for fourteen months, traveling regularly through the circuits and administering the ordinances in every place where it was convenient.

Mr. Wesley's plans for the American Church were somewhat changed at the General Conference held in Baltimore, May 1, 1787.   Mr. Wesley had communicated the following plan to Dr. Coke just before he left England to come to America.   The letter follows:

London, September 7, 1786.

Dear Sir:

I desire that you would appoint a General Conference of all our preachers in the United States to meet at Baltimore on May 1, 1787, and that Mr. Richard Whatcoat may be appointed Superintendent with Mr. Francis Asbury.

I am, dear sir,

Your affectionate friend and brother,
JOHN WESLEY.

To the Rev. Dr. Coke.

In addition to the request that Whatcoat be appointed Superintendent in the United States, John Wesley also nominated Freeborn Garrettson for the superintendency of the British possessions in America. The conference was called by Thomas Coke, at Baltimore, for May 1, 1787.   Several of the conferences had agreed upon this plan of John Wesley's for the American Church, but at the Virginia conference opposition was made toward the election of Richard Whatcoat to the Episcopacy. This opposition was led by James O'Kelley, who did not agree with Mr. Wesley's selection of a suitable man for the position "on account of his age, and also that he was a stranger in the wilderness of America." It was decided upon that the matter should be settled by the General Conferenc at Baltimore, "on condition that the Virginia Conference send a deputy to explain their sentiments."

The national consciousness of the American Methodist Episcopal Church is now seen exerting itself in opposition to John Wesley's control.

Bishop Asbury and Bishop Coke arrived at Baltimore on May 1, 1787, to begin the stormy conference that severed the last cord of control of John Wesley over the new church in America. Although, at no time were they unkind toward John Wesley. They looked upon him as their father but the situation was such that they could not accept his dictatorship over the American Methodists. The social, economic and political as well as religious forces forbade it. Nominations to elect Richard Whatcoat and Freeborn Garrettson to the Episcopal office, were rejected by the conference and thereby the plans of Wesley failed.

The rejection of Whatcoat may be laid to Jesse Lee's reasons why he should not be elected: "(1) That he was not qualified to take charge of the connection; (2) that they (the members of the conference) were apprehensive that, if Mr. Whatcoat was ordained, Mr. Wesley would likely recall Mr. Asbury and he would return to England." This last objection was not without foundation for it was John Wesley's desire to have Bishop Asbury return to England.

In order that we may understand more fully the situation which faced this conference, (it must be remembered that the newly formed Church in America was not only growing rapidly but was also increasing in prosperity. When prosperity began to be evident among the various churches in America, we see a Nationalistic pride appearing in the midst of the Methodist preachers, as to the right and authority of John Wesley over American Methodism. In the mind of not a few of the Methodist preachers, is seen, at this time, the attitude of reforming the liturgy, doctrine, and discipline, given by the founder of Methodism. This was due to the fact that John Wesley claimed supreme rule and power over the Ministers and Members, according to the form of government given to the American Church, and he cordially received, namely, "Moderate Episcopacy," which is defined by the best authorities to mean supreme rule and jurisdiction. But there is more involved in this title than supreme rule and jurisdiction; it means responsibility too. None of the preachers could ask with any degree of consistency, "How John Wesley came to such rule, and such power, or jurisdiction?" His authority is self-evident, for in the first place, all the preachers introduced themselves in Wesley's name, using his method, forms, doctrines and rules. In the second place, the people who joined were received into the societies or churches as Wesley directed. In the third place, John Wesley was the rector of the parish: all his preachers were curates and assistants to him in Europe and America. Wesley took upon himself to bear their reproach. All their weaknesses in their Christian life and ministry were charged to John Wesley. He led them in and out at his own expense and sacrifices of character, so that he was compelled to say, "Who is offended and I feel not?" In all sincerity, John Wesley was their supreme ruler, and under the commands of Christ, his rules were landmarks, the stones raised as guide-posts for his children. These were the books of appeal to which preachers and all those who called themselves Methodists were to resort for protection and aid. All this could not be understood correctly by the nationally conscious Methodists who had experienced along with their country the great and terrible price which had been paid for a new birth of freedom.

Trailing in the wake of the events which brought about political independence, at this conference there came naturally the religious independence in the birth of the American Methodist Episcopal Church, and the severing of the last cord of English control. The young American Radicals were heard in this Conference making many wild and unfounded, as well as founded statements. They bitterly attacked Wesley and maintained that his power must be checked, lest it grow even to Popery.

A motion was made at this conference to remove John Wesley's name from the minutes. Now, the minutes were in the form of questions and answers. Question, "Who are the superintendents of our church?" Ans. "John Wesley, Thomas Coke and Francis Asbury."

Evidently, not feeling safe, they turned their attention to Wesley's son in the Gospel, Thomas Coke, fearing his influence and jurisdiction. He would undoubtedly still possess the supreme rule and it was supposed that he would abuse that power. This matter was discussed in such a desultory way that Thomas Coke, to free them from their fears, or pretended fears, pledged them that he would relinquish his power as superintendent, in so far as it respected supreme jurisdiction and supreme rule, and that he would claim no authority, but to preside when conference did convene. So he consented to become a mere moderator, rather than have his name left off the minutes. Seeing what they had accomplished so far, some were not fully satisfied, so they even asked more than his word; thus, in the following document, he gave them his bond for the fulfillment of his promise:

I do solemnly engage by this instrument, that I never will, by virtue of my office of Superintendent of the Methodist Church in the United States of America, exercise any government whatsoever in the said Methodist Church, during my absence from the said United States. And I do also engage that I will exercise no government or privilege in the said Church, when present in the United States, except that of ordaining according to the regulations and laws already existing, or hereafter to be made in the said Church and that of presiding when present in the Conferences, and lastly, that of traveling at large. Given under my hand, the 2nd of May, in the year 1787.

THOMAS COKE.

Witnesses: JOHN TUNNELL,
              JOHN HAGGERTY
              NELSON REED

The friends of the patriarch Wesley sat down in astonishment. Among them was Richard Whatcoat, knowing that the servant of God must not strive, but be gentle, even towards such as oppose. One wondered at his patience, and apologized for his not opposing the measure more violently; to him Whatcoat replied in the following letter:

Dear Brother,
The ninth of this month I received yours of the

fourth of January; I thank you for the freedom you take in expressing your mind to me, and admire the confidence you place in me, as appears from the proposals you make. I hope I shall always give you some cause to look upon me as your friend and brother in th good cause of religion; I should be sorry to wound or grieve you in any measure; but why such haste, my brother? did you come to this part of the world, purely to recover your health? or did you come to reform our Church? If the former, hath not Providence blessed the means: 'If the latter, why did you not expostulate with our Conference on the subject? It appears to me that we have more need to unite all our forces, and use all our ability to unite, build up, and strengthen those who do stand; also to purge the floor, than to make rents in the body; it is easier to make a breach, than to mend one; it is easier to separate than to unite.

As to our seceding from Methodism, or Wesleyanism, I bless God that we have not seceded further than we have;—as to Methodism, I trust we retain the essential part.

As to my sitting by, tamely consenting to iniquitous acts, (referring to the Conference where Mr. Wesley's name was left out of the minutes) I thank you for your apology; but why should I throw myself into the sea to calm the wind?

It is one thing to feel the wind pierce you; and another, cordially to consent to it. As to the cruelties (if they may be called so) that I have met with, they are not worthy to be named when compared to the blessings I have received.

I bless God, I have not had an hour's uneasiness since I left Europe, about coming to this part of the world; I bless God, I am perfectly willing to spend the few days I have to labour, in the connection I am joined with.

My dear brother, while we see diabolical spirits in others, and inveteracies thrown out, let us take heed that they do not enter into us. May the good Lord

bless you with the mind that was in Christ.
So prays your sincere brother,
RICHARD WHATCOAT.

Francis Asbury was even attacked by a man of
warm passions who spoke out for Wesley's side, saying
that he was favourable to the opinions of the majority,
"Yea, that the spirit of Oliver Cromwell was in him."
The one who made this attack upon Asbury withdrew
from the Methodist Episcopal Church, and wrote to
John Wesley giving the subject coloring enough to mis-
lead Wesley as to the correct action of the Conference.
This letter seems to have reached Wesley bfore the
Minutes of the Conference, between when the Minutes
arrived they seemed to confirm what the letter had related, and it all tended to grieve Wesley greatly. Some
of Wesley's friends had said that he had trusted Francis
Asbury too far before Thomas Coke could arrive in
England to let him know the truth about the American
situation.

In the midst of this trial, Wesley writes to his son
in the ministry, Richard Whatcoat, as follows:

Dear Brother,
It was not well judged of Brother Asbury, to suffer,
much less indirectly to encourage, the foolish step in
the last Conference. Every preacher present ought,
both in duty and in prudence to have said, 'Brother
Asbury, Mr. Wesley is your father, consequently ours;'
candour will affirm this in the face of the world.

It is highly probable, the disallowing me will, as
soon as my head is laid, occasion a total breach between the English and American Methodists. They
will naturally say, 'If they can do without us, we can do
without them.' But they would find a greater difference than they imagine. Next would follow a separation among themselves.

Well, whoever may disagree tomorrow, let you and

I live today. I am,
Dear Richard,
    Your affectionate friend and brother,
                                    JOHN WESLEY.

Further dangers were yet to be encountered. It was feared that this incident would create a division in the American church, and that some would create societies under Wesley's control. Others felt like being scattered, when the shepherd had received so heavy a blow from his friends. Even others would continue still recognizing Wesley as their authority. Concerning this matter Richard Whatcoat was asked to give his opinion and counsel. This letter which was found among his papers gives his replies:

Dear Sir,

I have looked over thine, which I received last Sabbath, as no answer was asked. I show thee a more excellent way: when men revile you and persecute you, and say all manner of evil of you falsely, for Christ's sake, 'rejoice, and be exceeding glad; for great is your reward in heaven.' 'Christ also suffered for us, leaving us an example that we should follow his steps; who, when he was reviled, reviled not again; when he suffered, threatened not; but committed himself to Him that judgeth righteously.

'Blessed is the man that endureth temptation; for when he is tried, he shall receive the crown of life, which the Lord, the righteous Judge, hath promised to them that love Him.' Thy soul is more to thee than all the churches in the world, and the government of thy spirit, than all the disputes in Church and State!

Need I ask thee, whether thy soul is as happy as it was before the separating spirit was raised? As to myself, I thank God that I am what I am.—May heavenly wisdom guide us through this world to the blissful regions of bright eternity.

Shall I say thine, the least of all the saints,
                                    R. WHATCOAT.

At this time another situation which arose did not help the cause of the American Methodists or better relationships with the English Methodists. Thomas Coke, in the midst of these troubles and disputes, thought of forming a union between the Protestant Episcopal Church and the Methodist Episcopal Church in the United States. Out of the passing gossip Coke had collected his fears, which were increased by the rumor that it was reported that Francis Asbury had said, "That Mr. Wesley was like Cæsar, he could admit no equal; and that he was like Pompey, would know no superior." These and other rumors in circulation had a tendency to make it appear that Francis Asbury was a factious man, seeking his own glory at the expense of others, desiring to break the last thread of English control over the American church so it would appear that he was the only "Father of the Methodists in America." The friends of Asbury believed these rumors unfounded and unjust. Nevertheless, the condition of the Methodist Ministers was very uncertain; there was no hope for support for themselves and their families, if they were not able to work continually. Thomas Coke foresaw this situation and thought of a union with the Protestant Episcopal Church as a means of conserving the progress already made by the Methodists. Coke, as the story of his life reveals, was willing to make any sacrifice for the cause of Christ. He had left all to preach the Gospel. With these warm feelings, and under the impression that the cause of the Redeemer might be advanced by the doctrine preached by Wesley and his preachers, he mentioned this plan to a friendly bishop of the Protestant Episcopal Church in America. He realized that the Episcopacy could be no other than moderate in the

BARRATT'S CHAPEL

This is the picture of Barratt's Chapel which was built in 1780, the
Cradle of American Methodism

United States. Likewise, Coke feared that a deviation from the present form would lead to further confusion and fanaticism. Another reason why he proposed this union might have been that it would afford a greater opportunity for a more general spread of the Gospel in the states. He had passed several times through the states from the North to the South, and had seen much of that country laid out into districts or parishes with several churches or meeting houses, nearly all of which were without ministers, or even supplies. The Church property was in decay and inevitably would be sold at auction if permitted to go on in this way. If such a plan could be agreed upon, there was something to be gained by the Methodists who were in need of salaries and church property, and it means the saving of all the elements of value for the Protestant Episcopal Church. Coke's plan of union was not without an element of truth because the proposed plan might have prevented what actually did happen. Already the Virginian conference had proposed to petition the legislature to sell unoccupied churches. There was no law at this time authorizing the sale of such properties. The state needed money; the congregations were scattered. In fact there was much in all the southern states to invite such a union. Here we see the same articles, the same creed, the same baptism, the same liturgy, the same faith, the same people, engaged to build up the old waste places. Coke saw that Methodism had the experienced men, and that the Protestant Episcopal Church had the property and means; so why not a union?

Bishop Coke revealed this plan to one of his preachers who said that it would grieve Bishop Asbury and many others if such came before the Conference. Thus, he destroyed his papers and dropped the subject. The minister to whom Bishop Coke had revealed his plan, told Bishop Asbury. Then the matter was taken up by those who were not so kindly toward Bishop Coke and John Wesley in particular, and they used it to their own advantage, making it appear that it was a plot of Wesley and that Coke was his representative. The whole subject gave Asbury much grief and sorrow when he remembered the letter Wesley had written Richard Whatcoat. After finishing his work, Bishop Coke left America on June 5, 1789 on the ship "Union" bound for Liverpool.

Here we get a glimpse of Whatcoat's power and influence when we are reminded of the fact that he was with Bishop Asbury in all his troubles, and saved him for further usefulness to the Church. Whatcoat stood true and loyal to both Wesley and Asbury in this hour, which might seem impossible unless we come to know and understand Whatcoat, this soul and "Saint of Israel." This is only one out of the many incidents where the spirit and influence of Whatcoat saved souls and even churches in the hour of crisis.

The conference met at Uniontown on August 22, 1788. Bishop Asbury says, "We felt great peace while together and our counsels were marked by love and prudence. We had seven members of conference and five probationers. I preached on First Peter 5:7, and Brother Whatcoat gave us an excellent discourse on 'Oh man of God, flee these things.' " The conference was brought to a close after four days.

Again on August 28th, Bishop Asbury says, "We came over the mountains along very bad roads. Brother Whatcoat and myself were both sick. We stopped in Simpkins' and were comfortably entertained."

Bishop Asbury and Richard Whatcoat arrived the next day at Barratt's where they rested for a few days. This incident happened, "We had left our horses at Old Town on the other side of the river," says Bishop Asbury, "but I thought it best to have them brought over, and so it was; for that night there were two stolen."

Bishop Asbury continued his journey through the South, and returned to Baltimore in time for the conference which was to meet on September 10th. Asbury says of this conference, "Our conference began in Baltimore, I chose not to preach while my mind was clogged by business with so many persons and on so many subjects."

At this conference held in Baltimore, Whatcoat was sent to serve again on the Eastern Shore as presiding elder over Cecil, Kent, Talbot, Dorset, Annamessex, Somerset, Northampton, Caroline, and Dover circuits. He remained in this vast field between six and seven months.

To illustrate the way the Spirit visited his labours, I wish to cite the following account of a Quarterly Conference held on April 26, 1789, in the old meeting house near my own home in Dorchester County, South of Cambridge, Maryland. "The Lord came in power at our Sacrament, the cries of the mourners, and the ecstasies of believers were such, that the preacher's voice could scarcely be heard, for the space of three hours. Many were added to the number of true believers."

This incident was not the unusual thing but even greater spiritual manifestations were experienced elsewhere. We cite the St. Michael's Quarterly Conference which states, "The power of the Lord was present, to wound and to heal." On the Sabbath following, at Johnstown, on Caroline circuit, there was yet a more glorious visitation of the power of the Spirit at a love feast. "The house was filled with the members of our societies, and great numbers of people were on the outside; the doors and windows were thrown open, and some thronged in at the latter. Such times my eyes never beheld before."

CHAPTER VIII.

ASBURY'S TRAVELING COMPANION.

During the latter part of May, June, July, and August, we find Whatcoat traveling with Bishop Asbury through Philadelphia, New York, the Nine Partners, and through New Jersey to Philadelphia again, and then to Fort Pitts. Whatcoat—leaving Bishop Asbury—attended the conference at Uniontown, and returned to Baltimore on the 15th of September. After that he took a tour through the peninsula, and returned to Baltimore to join Bishop Asbury for a trip to the South, by way of Virginia, North Carolina, and South Carolina, arriving at Charleston on February 11th, 1790, where they held a conference. From there they passed into Georgia for another conference on March 3rd. They fulfilled many preaching engagements in Georgia and North Carolina, and passed on westward into Kentucky by way of Tennessee. This was a very dangerous and thrilling adventure. There are many instances of this journey related by Bishop Asbury, but not mentioned by Whatcoat.

Bishop Asbury and Richard Whatcoat crossed Roanoke River. They passed through Warren, Granville, Wake, Chatham, Orange, Randolph, and Richmond counties, then into North Carolina. Bishop Asbury when he preached at Night's Chapel near Hedgecock Creek on the following subject, "My Grace is sufficient for thee," stated, "There was some quickening, and I was blest."

There were many hardships and tiresome hours while on this journey. For example, says Asbury, "It is no small exercise to ride twenty miles or more as we frequently do before 12 o'clock taking all kinds of food and lodging and weather too, as it comes, whether it be good or bad." Their lives were constantly in danger from the hazards of the journey as well as from Indian attacks. Asbury says, "I saw the hand of the Lord in preserving my life and limbs, when my horse made an uncommon start, and sprung some yards with me. It was with difficulty I kept the saddle." They continued their journey into South Carolina. which was a severe day's ride, "and called at the Beauty Spot: the beauty here has somewhat faded. the society is disjoining and in a poor state," of affairs. They continued on their way preaching and holding meetings which gave evidence to a little spiritual life.

Richard Whatcoat preached at "The Grove," Asbury following him with a short mesage. There was quite a spiritual awakening attending that meeting. At the close of the meeting, they spent the night with an old friend, "Having ridden 25 miles, we were weary and hungry, having a breakfast on tea at 8 o'clock and taking nothing more until 6 o'clock at night," says Asbury. "Lord help me to bear all things without murmuring or disputing."

They crossed in the night at Port's Ferry where they had to get out and wade in the shallow places. They continued their journey to Georgetown, where Whatcoat preached on the Sabbath, using the text, "In all places where I record my name I will come unto thee and I will bless thee."

They passed through Wapataw, continuing on to Charlestown, where they received the news from Baltimore and New York that a great revival had spread through both cities and about two hundred persons had been converted in a few weeks. They remained at

Charlestown ten days, where they held a conference. Whatcoat preached almost every night. Spiritual fervor and quickening attended each service.

Their journey continued by way of Edisto River and at Lynders, Bishop Asbury was not feeling well and Whatcoat preached in his stead. Traveling on, until they arrived at Chester, they held a meeting and "there came only two men and thy were drunk." It seems evident by this journey, that the religious life of these people was at a low ebb as Asbury says, "After riding thirty miles, through heavy sands we came to Dr. Fuller's. I am strongly inclined to think I am done with this road and people. They pass for Christians—a profit of strong drink might suit them. I was clear in not receiving anything without paying for it."

The spirit of Bishop Asbury is revealed in the following quotation, "Since Friday the 19th, we have ridden about 160 miles. I have been under various trials and exercises and have some dejected hours. This also shall tend to my humiliation and work for my good."

Leaving Campbelltown by way of Augusta, they passed into Georgia. Continuing their journey, preaching here and there, they arrived on March 10, at Grant, where they held a conference. It seems that the great problem which faced this conference was the deficits in the preachers' salaries, who received sixty-four dollars a year. The deficits amounted to seventy-four pounds for that year. Yet the spirit was very good, and a revival broke out during this conference; many people were saved. Asbury, having preached in the new chapel at Bibbs' Cross Roads, where he ordained Bennet Maxey to the office of deacon, spent the night at a Brother Herbert's where he was told that a poor sinner was struck with conviction at the grave of Brother Major and thought he heard the voice of God calling him to repentance. He was also told of a woman who sent for Brother Andrew to preach her funeral sermon while she still lived. Brother Andrew complied with this request. The woman was blessed by the message and died in peace.

In the midst of all the hardships, Asbury and Whatcoat were kindly entertained by the people wherever they went. They found a very kind and friendly feeling between the Presbyterians and the Methodists. On many occasions, they were permitted to preach in the Presbyterian churches and to use the Presbyterian ministers' horses for traveling purposes.

They continued their journey back through South Carolina, into North Carolina. This journey was made through an awful thunder, wind and rain storm. They arrived at Col. Graham's "dripping wet with rain." Bishop Asbury was seriously ill. Here Whatcoat preached a most excellent sermon on the subject, "The Kingdom of God is not in word but in power." Bishop Asbury notes in his journal the following thoughts as to this sermon by Whatcoat: "Not in sentiments or forms but in the convincing, converting, regenerating, sanctifying power of God."

Again we find them traveling through rainy weather by way of Gilbertown, Rutherford and Berk counties. They crossed Catawba River at Greenley's Ford and arrived at Mr. White's on John's River about 8 o'clock on the night of April 1, 1790. Bishop Asbury was still suffering from his previous illness. They left Mr. White's, traveling through the Laurel Hill and having crossed the mountain, they forded the Watauga

River at its head. This country was very dangerous because of the terrible storms and the Indians and wolves which frequented that region. They were now passing into the frontier regions of Stone Mountain in Tennessee, where the way was rough and difficult. They continued on their journey, returning by way of Virginia where they visited General Russell. We note that from December 14, 1789, to April 20, 1790, they had traveled on horse-back, 2578 miles. They spent a short while at General Russell's, holding meetings at his home, while waiting to continue their journey into Kentucky. Likewise, they preached at many frontier stations.

Richard Whatcoat relates this experience in his memoirs as follows: "As we journeyed towards Holston night overtook us, and we were shut in between two mountains. We gave our horses a little provender out of our sacks, and letting them loose, struck up a fire—but the thunder gust nearly put it out. The next day we pursued our journey toward General Russell's and there we were kindly entertained. After a few days' rest we traveled on to the last station, in the Grassy Valley, expecting to meet a company to conduct us through the wilderness, according to appointment; but no company was heard of, and the next morning our horses were gone. That day diligent search was made but no horses were found; so the next day we packed up our saddles and baggage, on Brother Henderson's horse, and returned ten miles into the settlement. After we had been there a little while, two boys followed us with our horses. We traveled about the settlement, and held meetings for a fortnight.

"One morning Bishop Asbury told me that he

dreamed that he saw two men, well mounted, who told him they were come to conduct him to Kentucky, and had left their company in the Grassy Valley. So it was: after preaching they made their appearance; we then got our horses shod, mustered some provisions, joined our company, and passed through the wilderness about one hundred and fifty miles. The first day we came to the new station; here we lay under cover, but some of the company had to watch all night. The next two nights we watched by turns; some watching while others lay down. As there was not a good understanding between the savages and the white people, we traveled in jeopardy; but I think I never traveled with more solemn awe and serenity of mind. As we fed our horses three times a day, so we had prayer three times."

Again we quote from Asbury's Journal, the following account of the dangers encountered on this journey:

"Our way is over mountains, steep hills, deep rivers, and muddy creeks; a thick growth of reeds for miles together—and no inhabitants but wild beasts and savage men. Sometimes, before I was aware, my ideas would be leading me to be looking ahead for a fence, and I would, without reflection, try to recollect the houses we should have lodged at in the wilderness. I slept about an hour the first night, and about two the last, we ate no regular meal; our bread grew short, and I was much spent.

"I saw the graves of the slain twenty-four in one camp. I learned that they had set no guard, and that they were up late playing cards. A poor woman of the company had dreamed three times that the Indians had surprised and killed them all; she urged her husband to entreat the people to set a guard, but they only abused him and cursed him for his pains. As the poor woman was relating her last dream the Indians came upon the camp; she and her husband sprung away, one east, the other west, and escaped. She afterward came back, and witnessed the carnage. These poor sinners appeared to be ripe for destruction. These are some of the melancholy accidents to which the country is subject at present."

They went on into the West as far as Lexington, near which place they held a conference. Then they returned East by way of Tennessee and North Carolina, and into Virginia, holding a conference at Petersburg, Va. They arrived at Baltimore after traveling, in fifteen months, more than six thousand miles.

Richard Whatcoat continued on to Philadelphia, in the latter part of August, and after visiting New York, returned to Philadelphia there to take up his duties as Elder. With great joy and happiness he served these people for nine months.

Methodism, due to several events that had taken place in England and America, had become somewhat nationalized by this time. First: the Revolution had ended, making the colonies forever separate from the British Empire; Second, the period of formation of the colonies into a union of states had been accomplished; Third, the American Methodists had severed the final cord of Wesley's control over the Methodist Societies; Fourth, the Methodists were a definite religious body, having final control over their own affairs and future destiny; Fifth, Wesley's death in the year 1791 was greatly mourned by the Methodists of America, but his passing was not to disturb the future progress of the Methodist Church in America, because she was definitely organized and capable of self-control; Sixth, Washington had been elected first President of the United States.

The year 1791 opened finding Whatcoat in Philadelphia; Asbury was visiting the southern societies where he met Dr. Coke on Wednesday, March 23. Dr. Coke, who had just returned from England, had suffered ship-wreck off Edisto River but landed safely and brought to the ears of Bishop Asbury news of what had taken place in England concerning the future of the American Methodists. James O'Kelley, of Virginia, wrote a letter to John Wesley concerning certain items which seemed to be points of controversy between himself and Bishop Asbury. Bishop Asbury, in the mind of James O'Kelley, was becoming too popular and was having too great an influence over the American Methodists. This influence, he felt, was a reflection on the influence of John Wesley over Methodism. For years O'Kelley had been a contender for the supremacy of Wesley's authority over American Methodists. Evidently, O'Kelley's letter had influenced the minds of Wesley and Coke with regard to the Methodist Church in America. Dr. Coke had been sent on this mission to America, bringing advice that a general conference be called together, to which Bishop Asbury conceded. This general conference was to be called for the sake of peace and unity among Methodists.

Having completed their discussion concerning the Church, Bishop Asbury continued his visiting of the societies in the South, having Dr. Coke to assist him in this work.

On the journey to the North, from the South, they received the news of John Wesley's death. Friday the 29th, 1791, Bishop Asbury says:

The solemn news reached our ears that the public papers had announced the death of that dear man of God, John Wesley. He died in his own house in London, in the eighty-eighth year of his age, after preaching the Gospel sixty-four years. When we consider his plain and nervous writings; his uncommon talent for sermonizing and journalizing; that he had such a steady flow of animal spirits; so much of the spirit of government in him; his knowledge as an observer; his attainments as a scholar; his experience as a Christian; I conclude, his equal is not to be found among all the sons he hath brought up, nor his superior among all the sons of Adam he may have left behind. Brother Coke was sunk in spirit, and wished to hasten home immediately. For myself, notwithstanding my long absence from Mr. Wesley, and a few unpleasant expressions in some of the letters the dear old man has written to me, (occasioned by the misrepresentation of others), I feel the stroke most sensibly; and, I expect, I shall never read his works without reflecting on the loss which the Church of God and the world has sustained by his death. Dr. Coke, accompanied by Brother C——, and Dr. G——, set out for Baltimore in order to get the most speedy passage to England; leaving me to fill the appointments. I had a large congregation at Sister Bombry's. In the afternoon I rode to Sister Waller's, making a journey of forty miles for this day. Next day I overtook Dr. Coke and his company at Colchester. Brother Coxe's horse being sick, I put my old horse in his place to carry them to Alexandria; where we arrived about three o'clock, after riding forty miles by our reckoning. At Alexandria Dr. Coke had certain information of Mr. Wesley's death. On Sabbath Day he reached Baltimore, and preached on the occasion of Mr. Wesley's death; and mentioned some things which gave offence.

Bishops Asbury and Coke continued their journey to Baltimore, where they held a conference. After the conference in Baltimore, Bishop Coke took his leave of America. Bishop Asbury says on May 16th, "I rode to New Castle, and had the last interview with Dr. Coke." Bishop Asbury continued his journey through Chester to Philadelphia, joining Whatcoat, where they opened the conference on the 17th of May. Bishop Asbury says of this conference, "We had a tender, melting account of the dealings of God with many souls, and settled our business in much peace." Bishop Asbury continues his journey to New York, where he arrived on May 26, 1791. He says, "Our conference came together in great peace and love." Whatcoat attended the conference in New York, and was appointed to John's Street Church of that city until September of the next year. He had a very satisfactory ministry in New York.

CHAPTER IX.

LATER SUPERINTENDENCY IN AMERICA.

At the conference in New York on July 19, 1792, Whatcoat was sent as presiding elder to the city of Baltimore. On account of sickness he was delayed in arriving at his appointment until November. After a long illness, he was able to attend the General Conference, which met in Baltimore on November 1, 1792. He had a wonderful pastorate here, finding a fertile soil among many old friends. His labors were greatly rewarded by many spiritual awakenings.

Whatcoat welcomed the coming of Bishop Asbury to Baltimore on October 30, to prepare for the opening of the General Conference on Nov. 1. Bishop Asbury's trip to Baltimore was made through a storm of rain from which he contracted a terrible cold. He says of this: "I came to Baltimore in a storm of rain. Whilst we were seated in the room at Mr. Rodgers, in came Dr. Coke, of whose arrival we had not word and whom we embraced with great love." Bishop Asbury says on the opening of the conference:

I felt awful at the General Conference, which began November 1, 1792. At my desire they appointed a moderator, and preparatory committee, to keep order and bring forward the business with regularity. We had heavy debates on the first, second, and third sections of our form of discipline. My power to station the preachers without an appeal, was much debated, but finally carried by a very large majority. Perhaps a new bishop, new conference, and new laws, would have better pleased some. I have been much grieved for others, and distressed with the burden I bear, and must hereafter bear. O, my soul, enter into rest! Ah, who am I, that the burden of the work should lie on my heart, hands, and head?

The following letter was sent to the conference by Bishop Asbury:

My Dear Brethren:—Let my absence give you no pain—Dr. Coke presides. I am happily excused from assisting to make laws by which myself am to be governed: I have only to obey and execute. I am happy in the consideration that I never stationed a preacher through enmity, or as a punishment. I have acted for the glory of God, the good of the people, and to promote the usefulness of the preachers. Are you sure, that, if you please yourselves, the people will be as fully satisfied? They often say, 'Let us have such a preacher;' and sometimes, 'we will not have such a preacher—we will sooner pay him to stay at home.' Perhaps I must say, 'his appeal forced him upon you.' I am one—ye are many. I am as willing to serve you as ever. I want not to sit in any man's way. I scorn to solicit votes. I am a very trembling, poor creature to hear praise or dispraise. Speak your minds freely; but remember, you are only making laws for the present time. It may be, that as in some other things, so in this, a future day may give you further light. I am yours, etc.

FRANCIS ASBURY.

The following statement reveals the spirit in which Bishop Asbury undertook his work.

"I am not fond of altercations," says the Bishop, "we cannot please everybody—and sometimes not ourselves. I am resigned."

Evidently James O'Kelley was very dissatisfied and likewise unpopular among the ministers by this time which is shown by the following quotation from Bishop Asbury's Journal.

Mr. O'Kelley, being disappointed in not getting an appeal from any station made by me, withdrew from the connection and went off. For himself, the conference well knew he could not complain of the regu-

Whatcoat Methodist Episcopal Church, Snow Hill, Maryland

lation. He had been located to the south district of
Virginia for about ten succeeding years; and upon his
plan, might have located himself, and any preacher, or
set of preachers, to the district, whether the people
wished to have them or not.

The general conference went through the Discipline, Articles of Faith, Forms of Baptism, Matri-
mony, and the Burial of the Dead; as also the Offices
of Ordination. The conference ended in peace, after
voting another general conference to be held four years
hence. By desire of my brethren, I preached on I Peter 3:8. My mind was kept in peace, and my soul enjoyed rest in the Stronghold.

Thursday, 15. I was comforted at the women's
class meeting. I appointed three prayer meetings for
them, Sisters K————, O————, and F————, to be
the leaders of them. If this is regularly attended to, I
think good will follow.

On November 18th, Bishop Asbury's cold does not
seem to be getting any better, for he says, "having
taken cold, and had my rest broken, I went to bed to
bring on a free perspiration; and from this I received
relief, my soul breathed unto God; and I was exceedingly happy in his love. Some individuals among the
preachers having their jealousies about my influence in
the conference, I gave the matter wholly up to them,
and to Dr. Coke, who presided."

Whatcoat continued his work in Baltimore, where
he says, "After which I took my station in town, and
visited from house to house, and labored steadily until
the next conference, in 1793."

On November 21st, 1793, Bishop Asbury called the
conference session to order in Baltimore. He says, "I
was well pleased with the stations and the faithful talk
most of our brethren gave us of the experience and
exercises. I preached a charity sermon on, 'Hath God

cast away his people?' We collected 27 pounds which was augmented to 43 pounds and applied it to supplying the wants of the distressed preachers." He further stated that on Sunday the 27th, "I preached, and ordained elders and deacons at the Point, and at night in town, spoke on Jeremiah 9:12-14."

Richard Whatcoat was sent from the Baltimore district again to the Eastern Shore of Maryland and Delaware as Presiding Elder of this vast territory, including Dover, Milford, Somerset, Northampton, Annamessix, Dorset, Talbot, Caroline, Queen Anne. Kent and Cecil circuits.

The conference at Baltimore on October 20, 1794, assigned Whatcoat to the Presiding Elder's office again over the same district, with some slight changes of boundary, where he had served in the same capacity in 1788. This district was very large, including all the eastern part of Maryland and a portion of Delaware. His labours were very much increased by attending forty-eight quarterly conferences within the year. Yet this year was visited by great success. A great revival broke out, which swept the peninsula. He speaks of it in the following: "We had large congregations and many blessed revivals in different parts of the district, and quarterly meetings were generally comfortably lively and profitable."

"Some things appeared of an extraordinary nature," says Whatcoat, "while many were suddenly struck with conviction and fell to the ground, roaring out in the disquietude of their spirits, or lay in a state of apparent insensibility, after a while starting up and praising God, as though heaven had come into their souls; others were as much concerned for a clean heart, and as fully delivered. I had to attend forty-

eight quarterly meetings in the space of twelve months
while on this district."

It was during the month of May, 1795, that Methodism lost one of its best friends, who resided within
the bounds of Whatcoat's district.   Bishop Asbury
states that on May 21st,

> We set out for Baltimore; the rain came on heavily;
> I have not felt nor seen such since the 6th of March,
> since which time I have ridden about one thousand,
> two hundred miles.   This day I heard of the death of
> one among my best friends in America, Judge White,
> of Kent County, in the state of Delaware.   This news
> was attended with an awful shock to me.   I have met
> with nothing like it in the death of any friend on the
> continent.   Lord, help us all to live out our short day
> to thy glory!   I have lived days, weeks, and months in
> his house.   O, that his removal may be sanctified to my
> good and the good of the family!   He was about sixty-
> five years of age.   He was a friend to the poor and
> oppressed; he had been a professed churchman, and
> was united to the Methodist connection about seven-
> teen or eighteen years.   His house and heart were al-
> ways open, and he was a faithful friend to liberty in
> spirit and practice; he was a most indulgent husband,
> a tender father, and an affectionate friend.   ,

This is true, likewise, of Whatcoat because Whatcoat, according to his Memoirs, had made many visits
to Judge White's home where he spent many enjoyable
hours with the Judge and his family.

We find Bishop Asbury on the Eastern Shore holding quarterly conferences, concerning which he states:

"June 13th, our friends were loving at the Dorset
quarterly meeting, but not very lively; however, there
was some stir in the love feast.   At eleven o'clock, we
had nearly a thousand people collected, but they are
awfully hardened.   We had a heavy time: I felt much

like what I suppose Jonah felt.   We were furnished richly with the comforts of life.   I came to the dwelling house of my dear friend Judge White (whose death I have already mentioned) : it was like his funeral to me.   I learned since I came here, and I think it worthy of observation, that just before he died, unknown to his wife, he had showed Samuel his son, his books, and given directions concerning his house, etc.   He then came to his wife, and said, 'I feel as I never felt before,' and gave certain directions concerning his burial."

We find Bishop Asbury visiting the churches on Whatcoat's district during the month of June.   On June 24th, Asbury says, (while visiting Whatcoat's district), "I spent part of the week in visiting from house to house, I feel happy in speaking to all I find, whether parents, children or servants; I see no other way; a common means will not do.   Baxter, Wesley and our Form of Discipline say, 'Go into every house,' I would go farther and say, go into every kitchen and shop; address all, aged and young on the salvation of their souls.   We surely cannot do less."

This statement of Bishop Asbury reveals not only the spirit of Bishop Asbury in his method of pastoral care, but likewise, the spirit and method of Richard Whatcoat.   They were always anxious to go further than the laws of Wesley required.   It was the spiritual fulfillment that brought peace and harmony to their lives.

Again we find Bishop Asbury visiting the lower section of Whatcoat's district.   "July 11th," says Bishop Asbury, "we came to Snow Hill, on Pocomoke River.   I called on the weeping widow Bowen, whose late husband, after being the principal in building a

house for divine worship, died in peace.   Here I met
about one thousand people; being unable to command
the congregation from the pulpit, I stood in one of the
doors, and preached to those who were out of the
house.   I rode eight miles to the seashore; when we
came near, we felt the cool sea breeze very powerfully.
I lodged with S. Evans, whose house I visited sixteen
years ago; here are two people above seventy years
of age, who have lived together forty-eight years."

The church here referred to by Bishop Asbury is
the Whatcoat M. E. Church of Snow Hill, Maryland,
which was built and dedicated to their then Presiding
Elder.   It was an outgrowth of the great revival which
swept the peninsula under Whatcoat's administration.

Bishop Asbury continues his journey North, visiting Whatcoat's churches.   We note that he stopped at
Middletown, Wilmington, and Chester, on his way
to Philadelphia.

Whatcoat attended the General Conference, held in
Baltimore, October 20, 1796.   This was a stormy
conference because of the controversial elements that
still remained, as to Wesley's authority over the
American Methodists.   Bishop Asbury says of this
conference:

We came to Baltimore, where about a hundred
preachers were met for general conference.   They
agreed to a committee, and then complained; upon
which we dissolved ourselves.   I preached on "The
men of Issachar that knew what Israel ought to do;"
and again on, "Neither as being lords over God's heritage, but being ensamples to the flock:" there were
souls awakened and converted.   No angry passions
were felt amongst the preachers; we had a great deal
of good and judicious talk.   The conference rose on
Thursday, the 3rd of November; what we have done is

printed. Bishop Coke was cordially received, as my friend and colleague, to be wholly for America, unless a way should be opened to France. At this conference there was a stroke aimed at the president eldership. I am thankful that our session is over. My soul and body have health, and have hard labour. Brother Whatcoat is going to the south of Virginia, Brother M'Claskey is going to New Jersey, Brother Ware to Pennsylvania, and Brother Hutchinson to New York and Connecticut: very great and good changes have taken place.

"The entire work was now divided into six yearly conferences of greater territorial extent than the numerous 'district' conferences, which had been held annually for the convenience of the preachers in various parts of the country, but which had borne no distinctive names and had received no defined territorial limits. These six conferences were the New England, Philadelphia, Baltimore, Virginia, South Carolina and Western."

We find that the old controversy between Bishop Asbury and James O'Kelley was refreshed in the mind of Bishop Asbury while visiting the Societies and old friends in Virginia, where James O'Kelley had served. This is seen in the following note taken from his Journal on November 28th, 1796, which reads as follows:

I had solemn thoughts while I passed the house where Robert Williams lived and died, whose funeral rites I performed. I was amazed to hear that my dear aged friend, Benjamin Evans, now gone to glory, was converted to the new side by being told by J. O'Kelley that I had offended Mr. Wesley, and that he being about calling me to account, I cast him off altogether. But, query, did not J. O'Kelley set aside the appointment of Richard Whatcoat? And did not the Conference in Baltimore strike that minute out of our Discipline which was called a rejecting of Mr. Wesley? and now does J. O'Kelley lay all the blame on me? It is true, I never approved of that binding minute. I did not think it practical expediency to obey Mr. Wesley at three thousand miles distance, in all matters relative to church government, neither did Brother Whatcoat nor several others. At the first General Conference, I was mute and modest when it passed, and I was mute when it was expunged. For this Mr. Wesley blamed me, and was displeased that I did not rather reject the whole connection, or leave them, if they did not comply. But I could not give up the connection so easily after laboring and suffering so many years with and for them. After preaching at Jolliff's, we rode to Portsmouth, and preached in the evening where we had many people at a short warning. My subjects this day were 1 John 1:3, 4, and Isaiah 1:9.

At the conclusion of this conference, Whatcoat accompanied Bishops Asbury and Coke to Virginia, preaching here and there, and attending with them a conference held at Mobry's Chapel, on November 15, 1796. He then went to his new field of endeavor, as Presiding Elder over the south district of Virginia, to which he had been appointed by Bishop Asbury and Bishop Coke.

Bishop Asbury states in his Journal for December 7th: "I parted with my dear Brother Whatcoat, after travelling together for about 700 miles. It was painful to part, yet I was well pleased he had not to drive the rough way, and that through the rain. In this I loved my brother better than myself."

This district, like all others in its day, was very large. Whatcoat was able to make a round on this district once in three months. He would cover from six to seven hundred miles, and would pass through thirty counties in Virginia and North Carolina. At this period, Methodism was performing a great and wondrous work in that part of the country. "We had," says Whatcoat, "a great revival in several parts of this district; but the slave trade seems to hinder the progress of Christianity in these regions."

We note that on April 15th, 1798, during the session of the conference at Salem, Asbury says, "I appointed my dear, aged and faithful Brother Whatcoat to visit the four districts belonging to the Virginia Conference and wrote my apology as not being able to ride on horseback as heretofore,"

In August and September, 1798, Whatcoat visited Caswell, Tar River, Goshen, Newbern, Contenteny, Pamlico, and Roanoke circuits on James Rodger's district in North Carolina. On this tour he found many faithful souls and made many friends.

We find Richard Whatcoat attending the conference in Baltimore, which met on October 9, 1798. Asbury says in his Journal of October 25th. "In company with my never failing friend—as far as man can be so— Richard Whatcoat, I came to Roper's. My horse was taken sick, which detained me."

On October 13, 1799 Whatcoat returned to the Virginia district, and continued his work until April of the next year. Then he rode with Jesse Lee and Wm. McKendree to Maryland and attended the conference held at Robert Carnan's on the first of May. At this conference five were oidained to Elders' orders and one to the deacon's office. The conference having closed, they continued on to Baltimore to attend the General Conference.

CHAPTER X.

On May 6, the General Conference of 1800 opened its session in Baltimore, and continued to the 20th of the same month. There was an enormous amount of work to be done at this conference and several important questions to be decided. The one of major importance in this paper is concerning the physical health of Bishop Asbury which was preventing him from carrying on this tremendous task of supervising the Methodist Episcopal Church in America. Likewise, the British Conference had asked for Bishop Coke's services for the prosecution of their missionary work connected with that conference.

Bishop Asbury, finding it difficult to carry on, but not willing to retard the work, either in fact or in the estimation of his brethren, had seriously thought of resigning from office, and had even prepared a letter to that effect. When the subject came forth on the floor of the conference, and he had presented to them his situation, they were unwilling to lose his services, and passed two resolutions as the "sense of the conference," the second of which was as follows:

"This conference does earnestly entreat Mr. Asbury for a continuation of his services as one of the general superintendents of the Methodist Episcopal Church as far as his strength will permit."

They granted the request of the British Conference for the services of Bishop Coke. With these two matters disposed of, they set about to solve the problem of superintendency of the Church Coke supplied. It was agreed upon to elect another bishop, and to consecrate him at that conference. Here, another problem presented itself. Some contended that he should be an assistant only, and some, that he should be equal in power with his seniors. The latter contention prevailed.

They now set about to ballot for a bishop. On counting the first ballot, it was found that it was a tie between Richard Whatcoat and Jesse Lee, and a second ballot was necessary. The result of the second ballot was, fifty-nine votes for Richard Whatcoat, and fifty-five for Jesse Lee. Richard Whatcoat was therefore, declared elected to the office of bishop. On the 18th of May he was consecrated to the Episcopacy by the imposition of the hands of Bishop Asbury and Bishop Coke, assisted by a number of elders selected for the purpose. Whatcoat says in his Memoirs that, "I was elected and ordained to the Episcopal Office," which is characteristic of the Christian humility which he practiced. Bishop Coke preached the sermon on the occasion of the ordination of Bishop Whatcoat on the text: "And unto the Angel of the Church in Smyrna write; these things saith the first and the last, which was dead, and is alive."

This is the lad who was disturbed and troubled over death and eternity. He was honest with himself and faced these great problems with a determination to win —as he had faced all other problems since. That steadfastness had won the confidence of his brethren who had honoured him with the highest office and honour of the Church. The election was a closely contested one; and when we consider his competitor, it is still more evident that their confidence in him was unbounded. Jesse Lee had been one of the favorite preachers of Methodism in America. He was the recognized founder of Methodism in the New England

States, and moreover a native born American.

Francis Asbury dismisses this General Conference with a few lines in his Journal on May 5, 1800, but he gives an excellent account of what took place as follows:

We opened our General Conference, which held until Tuesday 20. We had much talk, but little work; two days were spent in considering about Dr. Coke's return to Europe, part of two days on Richard Whatcoat for a bishop, and one day in raising the salary of the itinerant preachers from $64.00 to $80.00 per year. We had one hundred and sixteen members present. It was still desired that I should continue in my station. On the eighteenth of May, 1800, Elder Whatcoat was ordained to the office of a bishop, after being elected by a majority of four votes more than Jesse Lee. The unction that attended the word was great; more than one hundred souls, at different times and places, professed conversion during the sitting of conference. I was weary, but sat very close in Conference.

Richard Whatcoat had thought it an honor to be ordained a deacon, as St. Stephen was, and an Elder, as the seventy; he had given to both the best that was in him. Now had come the crowning day. He was ordained a bishop, which was to him, an order of God. His life had proven the lines of the poet:

> To patient faith the prize is sure,
> And all that to the end endure
> The cross, shall wear the crown.

To this task he gave himself with all faith and sincerity, as he had given himself always before to the mission of shepherding and saving souls.

During the General Conference session of 1800, there had been much good accomplished by the ministers; and a great revival had commenced in the old part of Baltimore. Bishop Whatcoat says: "We had a most blessed time, and much preaching, fervent prayers, and strong exhortations through the city, while the high praises of a gracious God, reverberated from street to street, and from house to house, greatly alarming some of the citizens. It was thought that not less than two hundred were converted during the sitting of our conference."

Stevens says, "The General Conference of 1800 was one of the most remarkable in the history of our Church. The revival at that time was the greatest that has ever occurred during the session of any General Conference. I was a visitor, and had peculiar opportunities to witness the wonderful scenes that created joy on earth and in heaven. All the accounts we have had are extremely meager. As I have been preserved, while all who were actors in those scenes are gone, I will describe what I heard and saw at that time. It is not generally known that the greatest displays of divine power, and the most numerous conversions, were in private houses in prayer meetings. And yet the preaching was highly honored of God, for the ministers were endued with power from on high. I kept in my Journal a particular account of their texts and themes. The General Conference commenced its session Tuesday, May 6, in Light-street, Baltimore. All the General Conferences, from the famous Christmas Conference to the first delegated Conference, were held in Baltimore. Baltimore was a small place to what it is now. We then called it Baltimore town. The Methodists had two church edifices, one in Light-street, the other in Oldtown, which was in the suburbs. This was the first time I had ever seen a body of Methodist preachers; only now and then one wended his way to my father's neighborhood. The Conference was then composed of all traveling elders. The strong men of Methodism were there, and such a noble class of men I had never beheld. There were Philip Bruce, Jesse

Lee, George Roberts, John Bloodgood, William P. Chandler, John M'Claskey, Ezekiel Cooper, Nicholas Snethen, Thomas Morrell, Joseph Totten, Lawrence M'Combs, Thomas F. Sargent, William Burke, William M'Kendree, and others. These were representative men, who laid the broad foundations of Methodism east, west, north, and south. What a privilege to hear them debate, and listen to their sermons! Such was the health of Bishop Asbury that he thought of resigning; but the Conference, in order to relieve him, authorized him to take an elder as a traveling companion. They elected Richard Whatcoat bishop, he having a majority of four votes over Jesse Lee. I witnessed the excitement attending the different ballotings. The first, no election; the second, a tie; the third, Richard Whatcoat was elected.

The conference adjourned with a splendid feeling of harmony and a burning Spiritual Awakening within their souls to take to their new fields of labor. For the fields were already ripe unto harvest and reaping had begun in many places.

At this time a great revival commenced, the influence of which extended into almost all portions of the country, quickening the religious life and increasing churches. The dark and trying period through which the country passed at the beginning of its national life has been revealed to be one of such moral and spiritual desolation that many influential citizens were alarmed over the future prospects of Christianity. Days of fasting and prayer were observed annually, quarterly, monthly or weekly, varying in different localities, with earnest intercession that God would intercede in behalf of his suffering cause. It was due to this revival that the floods of infidelity and immorality were turned back. Likewise, it gave birth to numerous powerful religious and reforming agencies such as, The Bible,

Tract, Educational Foreign and Home Missionary Societies. These all came into being within the first twenty years of this century, as the outgrowth of the new life infused by this revival. It is interesting to note that the revival had its origin on the remote frontiers, in that portion of Kentucky and Tennessee lying west of the Cumberland Mountains, then known as the "Cumberland Country." This new country had attracted settlers from Virginia, the Carolinas and elsewhere. It was these people, who, finding life hard and difficult, felt the need of a greater power in their life, and began seeking for God and His aid in establishing their new homes. Like a wave, the new spiritual life rose beyond the Alleghenies, and rolling over the mountains, swept onward to the Atlantic and to the North. This frontier population was chiefly Presbyterians, Methodists, and Baptists. The preaching at this time, in most communities, consisted principally of dry discourses upon a stiff and technical theology, or a cold, speculative orthodoxy, which led to no warming of the heart or conviction of sin, nor change of life. Persons of quiet and orderly lives were received into the church membership without a religious experience.

There were five ministers who seemed to have an active part in the starting of this revival, three Presbyterians and two Methodists. Of the former were, James Gready, William McGee and Hodge; of the latter, John McGee and William Burke. The McGees were brothers. In the latter part of 1799 the two McGee brothers, one a Methodist and the other a Presbyterian, started upon a preaching mission from Tennessee into Kentucky. Their meetings, everywhere they went, were attended with remarkable demonstrations of the Spirit and revivals broke out, which went like fire from one community to another. At a meeting held at Muddy River, many families came for miles around in wagons and camped in the woods. This was the beginning of the "Camp Meeting" in this country which has since become an important religious institution. Bangs tells of a meeting held at Cobbin, Kentucky, that "twenty thousand persons were present" and that thousands fell as if slain in battle and its influence was felt throughout the state."

An eye witness thus writes concerning it:—

Few, if any, escaped without being affected. Such as tried to run from it, were frequently struck on the way, or impelled by some alarming signal to return. No circumstance at this meeting appeared more striking than the great numbers that fell on the third night; and to prevent their being trodden under foot by the multitude, they were collected together and laid out in order, or on two squares of the meeting house, till a considerable part of the floor was covered. But the great meeting at Caneridge exceeded all. The number that fell at this meeting was reckoned at about three thousand, among whom were several Presbyterian ministers, who, according to their own confession, had hitherto possessed only a speculative knowledge of religion. Here the formal professor, the deist, and the intemperate, met with one common lot, and confessed, with equal candor, that they were destitute of the true knowledge of God, and strangers to the religion of Jesus Christ.

William McKendree was presiding elder over this district and Fry says that "No small part of the impetus which was given to the work was by his preaching and superior wisdom."

We have seen McKendree tending westward for some years among the mountain appointments of Western Virginia, and witnessed his departure on his transmontane route with Asbury and Whatcoat, without his 'money, books, or clothes.' They passed over the mountains, down the Holston River, into Tennessee, into the valley of Church River, where, reaching a 'station' on the outskirts of the settlements, they combined with other travelers to form a company, and, on the 27th of September, 1800, began their course direct to Kentucky. Wearied and sick, they reached Bethel Academy, Jessamine County, and there held the Western Conference in the first week of October, the first session of that body of which there remains any correct record. Ten traveling preachers were present, including Asbury and Whatcoat; the session lasted but two days; two candidates were admitted on probation, one member located, fourteen local and four traveling preachers were ordained. Some of the members of the small body lingered long in the Church, but all have gone now to their rest.

After the session Asbury, Whatcoat, and McKendree traveled and preached together, from the center of Kentucky to Nashville, in Tennessee, and thence to Knoxville, where they parted, McKendree returning to his great district, which comprised thirteen circuits, over which he went preaching night and day with an ardor befitting so grand a sphere, and such sublime results as he could justly anticipate for the rising commonwealths around him, whose moral foundations Methodism was now effectively laying. An extraordinary religious excitement spread over all the country. It was largely attributable to the introduction of camp meetings at this time—a provision which, however questionable in dense communities, seemed providentially suited to these sparsely settled regions. In the latter part of 1799, John and William McGee, who were brothers, the first a Methodist local preacher, the second a Presbyterian minister, started from their settlement in Tennessee to make a preaching tour into Kentucky.

The following quotations are given from reliable sources as testimony to the extent and influence of this great revival. The first one is taken from a letter written by George A. Baxter, D. D., of Washington Academy, Virginia, who visited Kentucky in 1801, and personally inquired into the character of the revival; he writes to Dr. Archibald Alexander as follows:

On my way I was informed by settlers on the road that the character of Kentucky travelers was entirely changed, and that they were as remarkable for sobriety as they had formerly been for dissoluteness and immorality. And indeed I found Kentucky, to appearance, the most moral place I had ever seen. A profane expression was hardly ever heard. A religious awe seemed to pervade the country.

. . . . . Upon the whole, I think the revival in Kentucky the most extraordinary that has ever visited the Church of Christ; and, all things considered, it was peculiarly adapted to the circumstances of the country into which it came. Infidelity was triumphant and religion was on the point of expiring. Something extraordinary seemed necessary to arrest the attention of a giddy people who were ready to conclude that Christianity was a fable and futurity a delusion. This revival has done it. It has confounded infidelity and brought numbers beyond calculation under serious impressions.

The revival moved rapidly into New England and soon became more extensive in the Western New England. The Rev. Bennett Tyler, D. D., said:

Within the period of five or six years, commencing with 1797, not less than one hundred and fifty churches in New England were visited with 'times of refreshing from the presence of the Lord.'

Reverend Edward D. Griffin said:

I could stand in my door at New Hartford, Litchfield County, Connecticut, and number fifty or sixty contiguous congregations laid down in one field of Divine wonders, and as many more in different parts of

New England.

In a summary of the effects and influence of the revival of 1797 to 1803, the following testimonies are cited: Dr. Gardner Spring says:

From the year 1800 down to the year 1825 there was an uninterrupted series of these celestial visitations spreading over different parts of the land. During the whole of these twenty-five years there was not a month in which we could not point to some village, some city, some seminary of learning, and say, 'Behold, what hath God wrought!'

Dr. Herman Humphrey, a member of Yale College in 1802 says:

In looking back fifty years and more the great revival of that period strikes me in its thoroughness, in its depth, in its freedom from animal and unhealthy excitement, and its far-reaching influence on subsequent revivals, as having been decidedly in advance of any that had preceded it. It was the opening of a new revival epoch, which has lasted now more than half a century, with but short and partial interruptions—and, blessed be God, the end is not yet. The glorious cause of religion and philanthropy has advanced till it would require a space that cannot be afforded in these sketches so much as to name the Christian and humane societies which have sprung up all over our land within the last forty years. Exactly how much we at home and the world abroad are indebted for these organizations, so rich in blessings, to the revivals of 1800 is impossible to say, though much every way—more than enough to magnify the grace of God in the instruments he employed, in the immediate fruits of their labors, and the subsequent harvests springing from the good seed which was sown by the men whom God delighted thus to honor. It cannot be denied that modern missions sprung out of these revivals. The immediate connection between them, as cause and effect, was remarkably clear in the organization of the first societies, which have since accomplished so much; and the impulse which they gave to the churches to extend the blessings which they were diffusing by forming the later affiliated societies of like aims and character is scarcely less obvious.

CHAPTER XI.

INTRODUCTION TO THE EPISCOPACY.

It was in the midst of this great revival that Richard Whatcoat began his work as a Bishop of the Methodist Episcopal Church. Whatcoat felt right at home in a revival, because he was himself an Evangelical preacher and revivals attended his work everywhere he went.

The Bishops began their work at once, traveling together. They visited Abingdon on May 23, where Asbury says: "We came to Abingdon; the bricks are fallen down; the probability is we shall not rebuild with hewn stones. My text was Isa. 40:10, 'Behold, the Lord God will come with strong hand, and his arm shall rule for him: behold, his reward is with him, and his work before him.' This text was given me by opening my Bible at the sitting of the General Conference, when I trembled a little for the ark. The people have improved the chapel here. It was not burned with the college, although it was within twenty yards. We lodged at William Smith's; it is above twenty years since I lodged at his father's house."

On the first of June, about two weeks after the adjournment of the General Conference, we find them holding a conference, at the Duck Creek cross roads, now Smyrna, Delaware. This was a fine conference for everyone. Asbury says:

June 1. This was a day to be remembered. We began our love feast at half past eight; meeting was continued, except one hour's intermission, until four o'clock, and some people never left the house until nearly midnight; many souls professed to find the Lord. In the evening I rode up to Duck Creek, to meet the Conference.

June 2. We had sixty-six preachers, all connected with the business of Conference. We sat closely six hours each day, until Friday, 6, when about nine o'clock the Conference rose. One hour was spent in public each day, but the people would not leave the house day nor night; in short, such a time hath been seldom known. The probability is, that above one hundred souls were converted to God. The stationing of the preachers was a subject that took my attention. It was with the greatest difficulty I could unbend my mind from this one hour, yea, many minutes, by day or night, until I read the plan.

There were over one hundred persons converted and one hundred and fifty added to the membership of the church. Whatcoat says:

This was a glorious time; such a spirit of faith, prayer, and zeal, rested on the preachers and people, that I think it exceeded anything of the kind I ever saw before. O, the strong cries, groans, and agonies of the mourners! enough to pierce the hardest heart; but when the Deliverer set their souls at liberty, their ecstasies of joy were inexpressibly great, so that the high praises of the Redeemer's name sounded through the town, until solemnity appeared on every countenance: the effect of which was, that on the Thursday following, one hundred and fifteen persons joined the society in that town, while the divine flame spread greatly through the adjacent societies. We visited our societies, and passed on through Philadelphia.

Such awakenings were not unusual at annual conferences in those days. It was the purpose and mission of the conference to give an account of spiritual stewardship. Today it would be a miracle if a spiritual revival should burst forth at the seat of an Annual or General Conference.

Whatcoat omitted the following visit to Burlington, but Asbury says: "June 11. We rode to Burling-

ton, through excessive heat and dust, in company with
Richard Whatcoat and Jesse Lee; the latter wished to
preach in the evening, and so on in the morning. The
Baptist minister had appointed a lecture, and invited
Brother Lee to take his place; he accepted, and
preached an appropriate sermon on Acts 10:25."

They passed on to Philadelphia and from there to
New York, where they held a conference on the 19th
of June, 1800. Bishop Whatcoat preached at the ordination service in Bowry Church on the Sabbath, which
was a soul-stirring message to everyone present. Asbury gives the following account of this conference:

June 18. We rode in haste to New York, and on
Thursday, 19, we opened our Conference; about forty
preachers present. We had some knotty subjects to
talk over, which we did in great peace, plainness, and
love. Friday and Saturday we were closely confined
to business. Sabbath, my subject at the old church
was Rom. 12:19-21. In my introduction I observed
that the text was quoted from Lev. 19:18, and Prov.
25:21, 22, that it might discover to us what veneration
the New Testament writers had for the Old, and what
was required in a believer under that dispensation.
Vengeance is not our province; we cannot in civil,
much less in sacred causes be our own judges or
jurors. If we must feed an enemy, and not only forgive him an injury, but do him a favor, surely then,
we ought to love a friend, a Christian, and more
abundantly a minister of Christ. This day we made a
general collection for the support of the traveling ministry.

June 23. Our Conference concluded its sitting.
The deficiencies amount to $690; the moneys collected
and the draft on the Chartered Fund amounted to
$405. A motion was made to move the next yearly
Conference more into the center of the work, but it
was lost.

June 24. I have now a little rest. We have had a mighty stir in the Bowery Church for two nights past, until after midnight; perhaps twenty souls have found the Lord. Bishop Whatcoat preached the ordination sermon in the afternoon at the Bowery Church. I have now a little time to unbend my mind from the stations; but still my work is not done.

From New York they made a tour into New England. They held conferences at Lynn, Massachusetts, on the 18th of July, and fulfilled several preaching engagements at Boston and in Rhode Island and Connecticut, then returned to New York and spent a few days with Freeborn Garrettson, at his home on the Hudson River. Whatcoat says of this tour: "We pursued our course to the east through New London, Rhode Island, and Boston, to Lynn, in the state of Massachusetts; about five hundred and ninety miles, in the way we traveled. Here Conference began the 18th of July, and closed the 20th. There is a promising appearance of a good work in these eastern states. From hence we passed through Connecticut, New York, New Jersey, Pennsylvania, Maryland, Virginia, and Tennessee, to Bethel, in Kentucky, partly a south, and southwest course of one thousand, three hundred and twenty miles."

Asbury says:

July 4. The weather is damp and very warm. We came on to New Haven, where they were celebrating the Fourth of July. I fear some of them have broken good order, and become *independent* of strict sobriety. Bishop Whatcoat preached in the Sandemanian meeting house purchased by the Methodists.

July 11. We came to Preston, and were kindly entertained at Isaac Herrick's. It was the very height of rye harvest, yet many came together. I was greatly led out on the great salvation. I was refreshed in soul and body, and rode on in the evening to Nathan Herrick's. The simplicity and frugality of New England is desirable—you see the woman a mother, mistress, maid and wife, and in all these characters a conversable woman; she seeth to her own house, parlor, kitchen, and dairy; here are no noisy negroes running and lounging. If you wish breakfast at six or seven o'clock there is no setting the table an hour before the provisions can be produced.

July 15. We came to Boston. It was a damp day, with an easterly wind, unfriendly to my breast. As they were about finishing our church we could not preach in it. The new statehouse here is, perhaps, one of the most simply elegant in the United States. We made our home at Edward Haynes's, late from England, where we had most agreeable accommodations after our toil.

July 18. We sat in Conference at Lynn, Massachusetts. There were twenty-one members present.

July 19. The Conference rose, after voting the session of the next yearly Conference to be held at Lynn. And now the toil of six Conferences in seven months, and the riding of thirteen hundred miles, is over. I found some difficulty in stationing the married preachers.

July 27 (Connecticut). I preached at the new house in Thompson; my subject was Mark 8:34.

I observed: 1. The harmony of the evangelists Matthew and Luke with Mark; 2. That our Lord had given the clusters of the grapes of the promised land in blessings and promises; 3. He had given such demonstrations of his power upon the bodies of men: the dead were raised, the hungry fed, the lepers cleansed, the lame and the blind were restored, the wind and the sea were at his command; 4. He opened the distinguishing conditions of discipleship; the denial of self in every temper and affection that is evil. They that seek to save their lives by denying Christ shall lose soul and body; if it is through pride and shame Christ will not dishonor himself by owning such in the day of judgment.

August 1. Freeborn Garrettson came up with us. He attended the funeral of the Venerable Mother Livingston, who was suddenly and safely called home, aged seventy-eight, removed by a paralytic stroke, and probably it was apoplectic also. Perhaps it was about thirty-four years ago that this godly woman was awaked under the first sermon the Rev. Dr. Archibald Laidlie preached in the Reformed Low Dutch Church in New York, as she told me; nor she alone, but six or eight other respectable women.

Dr. Laidlie was born in Kelso, Scotland, December 4, 1727. He was the first English preacher among the Reformed ministers. His ministry in New York extended from 1763-1779. His influence was not confined to his demonstration.

Madame Livingston was one that gave invitation to the Methodist preachers to come to Rhinebeck, and received them into her house; and would have given them more countenance had she been under no other influence than of the Spirit of God and her own feelings. I visited her one year before her death, and spent a night at her mansion; she was sensible, conversable, and hospitable.

August 4. We came on and stopped at Goshen (New York) at Captain Wright's. The people flocked together at a short warning, and I gave a discourse on Isa. 35:3-6, after which we dined, and came on across the hills and over dreadful rocky roads to Cornwall, where Brother Whatcoat preached in the meeting house, on, "We know that we are of God, and the whole world lieth in wickedness."

August 5. We had another tolerable siege over the Housatonic River and hills to Sharon. Here Brother Whatcoat preached on, "The Lord knoweth how to deliver the godly out of temptations, and to reserve the unjust unto the day of judgment to be punished."

August 7. We came on to Freeborn Garrettson's new design, upon the Rhinebeck Flats. He hath a beautiful land and water prospect, and a good, simply elegant, useful house for God, his people, and the family. We have ridden between eighty and ninety miles since we departed from New York; and one-third of the roads were rocky and very uneven. I read a book of about five hundred pages, the author of which is a curious writer.

August 8-9. We regaled ourselves and horses upon the pleasant banks of the Hudson; where the passing and repassing of boats and small craft, perhaps fifty in a day, is a pleasant sight.

August 10. We had a sermon, and administered the sacrament at Brother Garrettson's; and notwithstanding public worship was held at the Dutch Church at the same hour, we had a large congregation. Bishop Whatcoat and myself filled up the service of the day.

August 12. We came through Poughkeepsie—no place for Methodism. We stopped at Elijah Morgan's; Brother Thatcher was preaching when we came in. We have ridden twenty-five miles this day, and dined in the road upon a watermelon that Mrs. Tillotson was kind enough to give us as we came by her house. I was so sick that I had but little appetite for anything else.

August 16. We pushed on with great courage, toward New York; but when within six miles of the city my horse blundered twice, and then came down with great force and broke the shaft. I got out, and my horse recovered from his fall. A smith's shop being at hand, the shaft was mended in an hour; and we came into New York and found our service was wanting in the city, there being here only two preachers, and one of them disabled.

August 26. We came into Maryland. Sometimes we had no roads, and at other times old ones that the wagons had left. Thus we bolted and blundered along the rocky rivulets until we came within sight of James Fisher's. The meeting had been appointed at the widow Jolly's; the house was large, and we had no small congregation; they came, some to see and some to hear. I had walked where I feared to ride, and it was exceedingly warm; but I took courage when I saw the people. The portion which I gave them was 1 John 2:24, 25. We had hardly time to eat and breathe before we had to beat a march over the rocks, eight miles to Henry Watters's, upon Deer Creek. Brother Whatcoat went ahead and preached, and I came on in time enough to exhort a little.

August 27. This evening we came with equal difficulties to Perry Hall, but the greatest trouble of all was that the elders of the house were not at home. The walls, the rooms no longer vocal, all to me appeared hung in sackcloth. I see not the pleasant countenances nor hear the cheerful voice of Mr. and Mrs. Gough! She is in ill health, and writes, "I have left home, perhaps never to return." This intelligence made me melancholy. Mrs. Gough hath been my faithful daughter; she never offended me at any time.

This journey reveals the hardships and qualities of the early pioneers for God in this country, and the uncertainty with which they traveled.

Whatcoat says of their visit to Nashville:

The 18th of October, 1800, William McKendree, Bishop Asbury, and myself preached at Nashville, (the capital of Cumberland settlement, finely situated on the banks of the river) to a large assembly; the word seemed to be with power; the 20th we attended the Presbyterian Sacramental occasion, held at Montgomery meeting-house, on Drake Creek, which continued four days and nights. After a short intercourse with the ministers, they desired us to take the stand, and speak to the people; accordingly brother McKendree, Bishop Asbury and myself spoke freely; the power of the Lord was present to wound, and to heal; several found peace that evening. It was truly pleasing to see so many gathered together, under the stately beech trees, to worship and adore the great Creator and Redeemer of mankind.

Asbury tells a little more of the detail happenings on their visit to Nashville:

October 19. I rode to Nashville, long heard of, but never seen by me until now. Some thought the congregation would be small, but I believed it would be large. Not less than one thousand people were in and out of the stone church, which if floored, ceiled, and glazed would be a grand house. We had three house public exercises. Mr. McKendree upon, "The wages of sin is death;" myself on Rom. 10:14, 15; Brother Whatcoat on, "When Christ, who is our life shall appear, then shall ye also appear with him in glory." We returned the same evening. I had a feeling sight of my dear old friend Green Hill and his wife. Who would have thought we should ever meet in this distant land? I had not time, as formerly, to go to their house to eat and sleep. We had a night meeting at Mr. Dickinson's.

October 21. Yesterday, and especially during the night, were witnessed scenes of deep interest. In the intervals between preaching the people refreshed themselves and horses and returned upon the ground. The stand was in the open air, embosomed in a wood of lofty beech trees. The ministers of God, Methodists and Presbyterians, united their labors and mingled with the childlike simplicity of primitive times. Fires blazing here and there dispelled the darkness, and the shouts of the redeemed captives, and the cries of precious souls struggling into life, broke the silence of midnight. The weather was delightful; as if heaven smiled, while mercy flowed in abundant streams of salvation to perishing sinners. We suppose there were at least thirty souls converted at this meeting. I rejoice that God is visiting the sons of the Puritans, who are candid enough to acknowledge their obligations to the Methodists.

October 25. I could not be content to leave the settlement without circumstantial account of the work of God, and I therefore desired John McGee to give it to me. And I purpose to select such accounts annually, and to read them in the large congregations, and then to have them published.

Bishop Whatcoat mentions the fact that they visited Knoxville. "We preached at several places, and passed on to Knoxville, where Bishop Asbury and I preached in the state-house, to a large assembly."

On October 29, Asbury seems to appreciate the hospitality shown them in the wilderness in the following lines:

We came to the new station at the Crab Orchard, where, although the station was not yet put in order, Mr. Sidnor received us politely, and treated us to tea. Here we found a cabin under the direction of the Cherokee nation, on land they claimed as theirs. Through camps and mud we pushed forward to Clarke's Ferry, upon Clinch, in sight of the fort at Southwest Point, at the junction of Tennessee and Clinch Rivers. We have traveled nearly seventy miles upon land belonging to the Cherokee nation. This Indian land cuts the state of Tennessee into two parts, passing nearly through the middle, making an indent upon the state of Kentucky on Yellow Creek. We arrived at Mr. Clarke's, where we received great entertainment. There was a good fire in the hall, and we were provided with a good dinner, and treated to tea. A fire was also kindled upstairs, at which we dried our clothes; to which may be added excellent lodging in two inner rooms. Thus were we within, while our horses were feeding to fullness in a grassy valley without. Our kind host rents the land from the Indians at six hundred per annum, himself making the improvements. It is a good arrangement.

On November 2nd Bishop Whatcoat says:

Brother McKendree closed the service with prayer. Bishop Asbury ordained John Winton to the Deacon's office, and baptized four children. The way we traveled from Nashville to Knoxville, Tenn., was about two hundred and twenty-three miles, partly a southeast course; but it was trying to our delicate constitutions, to ride through the rain a great part of the day, until late in the night, and then to encamp on the wet ground, the wind and rain beating hard upon us.

From Knoxville to Augusta, in Georgia, we took near a south course, of about three hundred and thirty-five miles. We preached at several places by the way; but oh, what mountains and rocks we had to pass over. When we came within a few miles of the Hot Springs, Bishop Asbury got a friend to lead his horse; but the road being rough and narrow, the horse stumbled or started, and turned the sulky bottom upwards, between the Paint Rock, French Broad River; but the horse lay quietly on his back until we released the harness; the carriage rested against a large sapling, which supported it from going down into the river. November 30th, I preached in a dwelling-house in the morning, and Bishop Asbury preached in the church in the afternoon, to a thin congregation: it looked like the "day of small things."

Asbury speaks of many events taking place on their tour up to January 1st, 1801, as follows:

November 4. Rode twenty, miles up Nollichucky to Benjamin Van Pelt's, where I had left my horse and chaise. From the twenty-seventh of last month, the day on which we left the pleasant mansion of our friend Van Pelt, to the day of our return, we rode, I presume, quite six hundred and sixty if not seven hundred miles.

November 14. On the sixteenth of September we set out from Virginia, and on the fourteenth of November we were in North Carolina. In this time I presume we have traveled one thousand miles, have had about twenty appointments, not many of which were large; have lodged about twenty nights under strange roofs, or at houses of entertainment; and have expended about $50.

November 23. An extraordinary cold day at King's Chapel. I began reading at eleven o'clock, and occupied the pulpit one hour and twenty minutes; Brother Whatcoat followed for fifty minutes, and Brother Blanton succeeded him; to this followed the sacrament—making the public exercises four hours, or thereabouts, of continuance, in a very open building. It may not be amiss to mention that this house for the worship of God was named after James King, who died a martyr to the yellow fever in Charleston.

November 29. (Georgia). Came twelve miles through deep sands to Augusta. We have traveled nearly one hundred miles since last Sabbath day. My soul hath been kept in great peace, but I feel the effects of riding a stiff, aged, falling horse, with a sore back, and my saddle is old and worn. Augusta is decidedly one of the most level and beautiful spots for a town I have yet seen. It is of ample extent in its plan, well begun, and when their intention shall be fulfilled of building a courthouse, a college, espiscopal churches for Methodists and others, it will do credit to its founders and inhabitants.

December 5. I humbled my soul before God. To-day I have been occupied in correcting a transcript of my Journal, that one had copied for me, who did not well understand my shorthand. The original was written in my great illness, very imperfectly; but when I reflect on my situation at that time, I wonder that it is as well as it is.

December 14. We had sacrament and sermon; my subject was Matt. 17:5: "This is my beloved Son, in whom I am well pleased; hear ye him." Introduction. These words were in part spoken at his baptism (see Matt. 3:17; Mark 1:2; Luke 3:22; that there were three witnesses present to hear, and four had recorded it—to wit, Matthew, Mark, Luke and Peter. 1. The Divine Father acknowledged the sacred and mysterious union—"This is my beloved Son:" a relation infinitely above that of angels, of Adam in his primeval standing, and the souls of any regenerated, sanctified, or glorified soul, on earth or in heaven—co-equal, co-eternal, and co-essential with the Father. "Well-pleased!" that is, in the whole of man's redemption by this "beloved Son;" "well-pleased"—in his preaching, living, dying—in every part of his official character. "Hear ye him"—Mark and Luke have omitted "ye." 2. The particular characters who should hear him in his word, Spirit, and operations. His ministers should hear him —this was designed in the text, by "ye:" hear him all his sanctified souls; hear him all who are justified; hear him all ye seekers; hear him all ye sinners, hear his awful warnings; all ye backsliders, hear him as Peter heard him, and repent, and turn to him; hear him ye apostates, as Judas, and despair.

December 21. I saw one of the members of the General Assembly of South Carolina, who informed me that our address from the General Conference had been read and reprobated; and furthermore, that it had been the occasion of producing a law which prohibited a minister's attempting to instruct any number of blacks with the doors shut; and authorizing a peace officer to break open the door in such cases, and disperse or whip the offenders.

CHRISTMAS DAY. At Glenn's Flat, Chester County, Sealey's meetinghouse, we kept our Christmas. Brother Whatcoat preached on, "The Son of God was manifested, that he might destroy the works of the devil." My subject was, "Glory to God in the highest, and on earth peace, good will toward men." We lodged at Robert Walker's, eighty years of age, awakened under Mr. Whitefield in Fogg's Manor, re-awakened at Pipe Creek and a member of the first Methodist Society in Maryland.

December 30. Came to Camden. I have received several letters from the North: they bring small consolation—'While he was yet speaking there came also another'—murmurs—complaints of partiality—and with this I may console myself in the midst of unremitted and hard traveling and labor. I was presented with a petition from about eighty male members of the society in the city of brotherly love, entreating me to do what I had no intention of doing—that was, to remove Brother Everett from the city. How, indeed, was this to be done? He and they had acquitted Robert Manley of the charges brought against him and restored him to membership; the presiding elder had also restored to office three or four elders who had been put out for murmurings and mischiefs, and had ejected the elder stationed in the city, and had filled his place by another—and they had great congregations, great shoutings; and God was with them, and nearly one hundred had joined the society. To all this what can we do but say, 'Well done, thou good and faithful servant' and servants! Poor Bishop! no money for my expenses. I am afflicted—my life threatened on the one hand, my brethren discontented on the other. True, I received from them a petition dipped in oil and honey; and if I approve, all will be well; but if not, drawn swords may be feared.

We find them, then, facing toward the west by way of Baltimore, Virginia, and Kentucky, then through Tennessee and Georgia and South Carolina, visiting the societies on their way and preaching whenever they were privileged. Whatcoat is very brief in his narrative as to what was going on in the south and southwest. Asbury tells of the following events:

August 30. Wilson Lee is all upon the wing in the work. Glory! glory! glory! I will not speak of numbers or particular cases without more accurate information, which in my haste I cannot now obtain; but without doubt, some hundreds in three months have been under awakenings and conversions, upon the Western Shore, District of Maryland.

August 31. Perhaps six hundred souls, in this district and in Baltimore, have been converted since the General Conference. Hartford, Baltimore, Calvert, Federal, Montgomery, and Frederick feel the flame.

September 9. We rode to Rivanna, in Fluvanna County: I have seen the hot, warm, sweet, yellow, red, and now have passed the green springs. When we came within six miles of Magruder's, Brother Whatcoat being in the carriage, the hindmost brace gave way. I took hold of a sapling by the roadside, and put it under the body of the carriage, and Brother Magruder mounted the horse, and we soon came to his house; that evening the breach was repaired. I took William McKendree's horse, and went on fourteen miles, to Richard Davenport's, in Amherst.

September 14. We rode sixteen miles to Liberty, and preached in Bedford Courthouse: I was sick in earnest. When I came up into the crowd, the people gathered around my carriage, as if I had had a cake and cider cart; this sight occasioned a kind of shock, that made me forget my sickness. After alighting I went immediately to the throng in the Courthouse, and founded a discourse upon Matt. 22:5. What great things the gospel revealeth to mankind. 1. The love of God; 2. The sufferings, and death, and merits of Christ; 3. The gifts, extraordinary and ordinary, of the Holy Ghost. Men make light of all the blessings of God, and of all the miseries and consequences of sin; they not only think lightly, but are opposed exceedingly to, them; 'for the carnal mind is enmity against God,' and the things of God.

September 29. We began our grand route to Kentucky at eight o'clock. We had to climb the steeps of Clinch about the heat of the day; walk up I could not: I rode, and rested my horse by dismounting at times. We came to Hunt's for the first night. Such roads and entertainment I did not ever again expect to see, at least in so short a time.

October 1. (Kentucky). We came to Logan's and fed. This low and new land is scented; I was almost sickened with the smell. I am not strong.

October 14. I came to Bethel. Bishop Whatcoat and William McKendree preached. I was so dejected I could say little, but weep. Here is Cokesbury in miniature, eighty by thirty feet, three stories, with a high roof, and finished below. Now we want a fund and an income of three hundred per year to carry it on; without which it will be useless. But it is too distant from public places; its being surrounded by the river Kentucky, in part, we now find to be no benefit. Thus all our excellencies are turned into defects. Perhaps Brother Poythress and myself were as much overseen with this place as Dr. Coke was with the seat of Cokesbury. But all is right that works right, and all is wrong that works wrong, and we must be blamed by men of slender sense for consequences impossible to foresee, for other people's misconduct. Sabbath day, Monday and Tuesday we were shut up in Bethel with the traveling and local ministry and the trustees that could be called together. We ordained fourteen or fifteen local and traveling deacons. It was thought expedient to carry the first design of education into execution, and that we should employ a man of sterling qualifications, to be chosen by and under the direction of a select number of trustees and others, who should obligate themselves to see him paid, and take the profits, if any, arising from the establishment. Dr. Jennings was thought of, talked of, and written to.

Dr. Samuel K. Jennings, a local preacher of Baltimore, afterward concerned in the "Mutual Rights" controversy.

Whatcoat says: "We held a little Conference on the 6th and 7th of October, 1800; the weather was unfavourable, and our stay very short; so that we had but little opportunity of seeing the country or people. As we journeyed on towards Nashville, in the state of Tennessee, partly a south course of about two hundred and twenty miles, we heard a strange report about religion. We were told that the Presbyterians work by new rules; that they make the people cry and fall down, and profess to be converted."

At Camden, South Carolina, they held a conference on January 1, 1801, and ordained several for the work of the ministry. "After traveling about two hundred and ninety miles from Augusta," says Bishop Whatcoat, "we came to Camden, in South Carolina, the 31st of December: here we opened our conference in Isaac Smith's house, the 1st of January, 1801, preaching every day: very few of the citizens attended, the weather being severe. We had great peace among ourselves, and were kindly entertained by two families. Seven preachers were received on trial, six located, five ordained to the Deacon's, and three to the Elder's office; Tuesday the 6th, we closed our conference in brotherly love."

Bishop Asbury gives a more complete account of this conference:

January 1, 1801 (South Carolina). We began our Conference at Camden with the new year. Sat from nine to twelve o'clock in the forenoon, and two hours in the afternoon; the band meeting was held between the hours of seven and eight. A clerk for the minutes was appointed, and another to keep the journal. We admitted four probationers; readmitted two deacons to their standing in the traveling connection, who had left it to locate; located three, to wit, Blanton, Cole and Evans, and restationed Gaines, Wiley and West, who had all located themselves in the course of the last year. We had great union. It is true, some talked loud, but I dare not say there was any improper heat. Our sitting continued five days, and we rested one Sabbath. We were richly accommodated at Smith's and Carpenter's, and two other houses. We only failed $48 in paying all the preachers their demands.

We passed on nearly in an east course; says Bishop Whatcoat, and stopped at Richard Green's, Kingston, near Little River, the 6th of February. I read a part of Prince's Christian History, containing accounts of the revivals and propagation of religion in Great Britain and America, for the year 1743; its features, tendencies, and effects were similar to what has appeared in our day; J. A. Robe, minister of the Gospel at Kilsyth observes that this caused the Rev. Mr. Edwards, minister of the Gospel at Northampton, in New England, to preach and publish a sermon on the distinguishing marks of the work of the Spirit of God; he also observes, there is much reason to conclude that the work of God in converting many in several parishes in the shire of Ayre, and other places, from 1625 to 1630, was attended with much the same appearance.

On January 12, 1801, Bishop Asbury says, "On this day we rested, and were busily employed in looking over our books and papers. I felt deeply affected for the rising generation. Having resolved to catechise the children myself, I procured a Scripture catechism, and began with Brother Horton's; to this duty I purpose to attend in every house where leisure and opportunity may permit."

January 18. Came to Wadesboro after a court week, says Bishop Asbury. We held our meeting underneath the courthouse, within the arches. We had a most delightful day. Bishop Whatcoat spoke with great ingenuity and authority upon 'The wages of sin is death; but the gift of God is eternal life.' My subject was Luke 18:27.

January 23. (South Carolina). We now descend into South Carolina. Marlboro County presents many interesting views, the sawmills, the solitary, lofty, long leaved pines, and the land, though barren, is of the most beautiful kind, and for range for cattle and for timber is very valuable. It was my lot to be speaker. Brother Whatcoat had taken so deep a cold he could do nothing. I preached from the parable of the sower.

Evidently there were ministers in the churches who were accusing Bishop Asbury and Bishop Whatcoat of partiality. On March 26 Bishop Asbury writes in his Journal:

I find reasons enough in my own mind to justify myself against the low murmurs of partiality in which some have indulged. We are impartial. We spend as much time in the extremities. We know not Maryland or Delaware, after the flesh, more than Kentucky, Cumberland, Georgia or the Carolinas. It is our duty to save the health of preachers where we can; to make particular appointments for some important charges; and it is our duty to embrace all parts of the continent and Union, after the example of primitive times and the first faithful preachers in America.

On January 30, Bishop Asbury seems to be distressed over the condition in South Carolina because he writes:

Sure nothing could so effectually alarm and arm the citizens of South Carolina against the Methodists as the "Address of the General Conference." The rich among the people never thought us worthy to preach to them. They did indeed give their slaves liberty to hear and join our church, but now it appears the poor Africans will no longer have this indulgence. Perhaps we shall soon be thought unfit for the company of their dogs. But who will mourn the loss of the friendship of the world that hath so hated our Lord and Master Jesus Christ?

The most striking feature of the Journal of the General Conference of 1800 is the persistent antislavery interest of many of the most eminent men in the Conference. Many resolutions were introduced, and a very decided utterance on the subject of negro slavery was made. This action aroused great hostility in South Carolina.

"We continued our travels," says Bishop Whatcoat, "through a level country, thinly settled, sandy roads, thick set with lofty pines; preached at several places. On the 25th of February, 1801, we dined at General Smith's and rode to Jesse Fenorett's, Wilmington; 26th, Bishop Asbury preached in the morning in the Methodist Episcopal Church, and in the afternoon in the Episcopal Church; 27th we traveled on, and came to Newbern the 6th of March; the way we traveled from Camden to Newbern, was about five hundred miles. We continued our course through a level, rich, but sickly country, preaching most days, and came to Portsmouth the 28th of March—from Newbern two hundred and twenty miles. After the exercises of the Sabbath, we took a west course of about one hundred and thirty miles, to Edward Droomgoole's."

Asbury says, "In a serious conference with Bishop Whatcoat, N. Snethen, Lyle, Hutchinson, and myself it plainly appeared that the best way in future would be to meet at the Virginia Conference; after which, one might go to the East, and the other to the Western Conference: the bishop who went East would then visit the Eastern states and the lake country, and thence onward to Pittsburgh and the Virginia Districts; the bishop who goeth West will visit over the Blue Ridge, Holston, Kentucky, Tennessee, Georgia, South and North Carolina, to the Conferences in the center of the work, where both will meet again. In this we all agreed. It was also determined that each bishop should always have an elder as a traveling companion."

On April 9th they attended the Virginia Conference, Whatcoat says: "April 9th, our Conference began; we had peace and good order; three preachers were ordained to the Elder's, and seven to the Deacon's office. After visiting several societies, we came to Petersburg on the 19th,—from Norfolk, the way we came, about two hundred and sixteen miles. We passed through Richmond, Fredericksburg, Alexandria, and Montgomery, to Pipe Creek. On the 1st of May our Conference began at Henry Willis's and closed the 5th, in great peace; six preachers were ordained to the

Elder's, and one to the Deacon's office.   After preaching at Ryster's Town, and the stone chapel, we came to Baltimore the 8th of May;—the way we came from Petersburg to Baltimore is about two hundred and sixty-six miles."

On arriving at Baltimore, Bishop Whatcoat completed his first tour of the Methodist Societies in his new office.

CHAPTER XII.

THE EPISCOPACY.

Bishop Asbury and Bishop Whatcoat continued their work of visiting the societies and holding conferences in the middle and eastern states until September. Bishop Whatcoat says:

"Conference began at Philadelphia on the 1st of June, 1801, and closed the 6th. We ordained six to the Elder's, and seven to the Deacon's office. Saturday, the 13th, I left Bishop Asbury under Doctor Physic's care; spent the Sabbath at Trenton, and on the 15th, rode towards New York. Our Conference began Tuesday, the 16th, and closed the 22nd, in great peace and harmony; I ordained eight to the Elder's, and four traveling, and two local preachers to the Deacon's office; the 23rd, started for the east, and passed over a hilly and stony country, thickly settled and much improved, through Reading, East Mountain, Hartford, and Boston, to Lynn, in the state of Massachusetts, preaching at several places by the way."

They began their Conference at Lynn, July 17th, and closed the 19th. "I ordained two to the Deacon's, and two to the Elder's office; we had great peace and harmony, preaching morning and evening, and four times on the Sabbath; the way we traveled from Baltimore to Lynn, is about five hundred and thirty-three miles. From Lynn we took nearly a northwest course of two hundred and twenty miles, to Ashgrove or Cambridge, in the state of New York, over a mountainous but fruitful country. Brother Hutchinson and I traveled on through Milton, Tioga Point, the English Station, Northumberland, Carlisle, Shippensburg,

Chambersburg, Green Castle, and Hager's Town, to Frederick, in Maryland, about five hundred and fifty miles from Ashgrove, through a country partly of wilderness, uneven, and mountainous, and partly thick settled and fruitful: we found a people to preach to in most places, more or less, by day or night. Bishop Asbury preached in Fredericktown the 28th of August; the 29th, he took his tour for Tennessee; and Brother Hutchinson and I for Georgia, through the midlands of Maryland, Virginia, and North Carolina."

About the first of September, Bishop Whatcoat, accompanied by Sylvester Hutchinson, took a southern trip as far as Georgia, where they were to meet Bishop Asbury and Nicholas Snethen, who had toured the West. However, they met in South Carolina about the last of October. Separating again, Bishop Whatcoat visited the churches eastward to Savannah, Georgia. Bishop Whatcoat says: "The 30th of October, we met Bishop Asbury, and were together a few days. November 1st, Nicholas Snethen preached morning and afternoon at Augusta, and I preached at night in our new church: the people were greatly attracted by Brother Snethen's preaching. The way we traveled from Frederick to Augusta, is about seven hundred and sixty-three miles."

They had now decided to travel separately, since Bishop Whatcoat was gaining sufficient knowledge of his new work to go alone, only traveling together whenever it was convenient to do so. They had now divided the work, which would make it less difficult. Bishop Whatcoat was given the southern route. Bishop Whatcoat says:

Brother Hutchinson and I took a south or southwest course, of about three hundred and thirty-seven miles, from Augusta to St. Tillers, through a sandy, pine part of Georgia, very thinly settled. We preached at one place where we were informed they had not had a sermon preached in the neighborhood for the space of twelve months. The 29th of November I preached in the meeting-house near John Crawford's, to about fifty or sixty people, from 1 John 3:9. From this place to Colerayn is ten miles, and to New Town, on the mouth of St. Mary's twenty-five; but the fever was there, and about thirty had died, we were told. From St. Tiller's to Savannah, we took near a south-east course, of about one hundred and sixty-six miles, preaching at eight places, and calling to see the ruins of the Orphan House. Oh, the waste of fifty years! What are men pursuing? How soon will worlds be thrown into ruins! I was kindly entertained at Mr. John Millin's, Savannah; the Rev. Mr. Holcom, and the Rev. Mr. Smith kindly offered me their pulpits for the Sabbath. I preached in the Baptist Church in the morning, and in the Presbyterian Church in the afternoon, the congregations were large and respectable.

December 15th, we passed on through a low, flat country for fifty or one hundred miles from the Sea Coast being much of it covered with water, and thinly inhabited, except by the negroes who work the rice fields. We came to Charleston, in South Carolina, the 18th of December,—about one hundred and thirty miles from Savannah. After spending ten days with the citizens, we rode to Camden, one hundred and thirty miles from Charleston.

Here our Conference began the 1st of January, 1802, and closed the 5th, in great peace. We ordained six to the Deacon's, and six to the Elder's office. On the 7th. Brother Hutchinson and I continued our course up the country, until we came to William White's, on John's Run, a branch of the Catawba; then Brother Hutchinson took his course for Kentucky, and I con-tinued my course through the hill country, until I came to Samuel Holmes', Mecklenburg, in Virginia. I preached nearly every day, and ordained eleven local preachers to the Deacon's office.

Our Conference began at Salem, March 1st, and closed the 4th. I ordained seven traveling, and five local preachers to the Deacon's office; it was thought that ten or twelve were converted during the sitting of our Conference; on the 7th, I preached at Petersburg, and ordained one local preacher to the Deacon's office; from Camden to Petersburg, the way I traveled, is about five hundred and eighty-five miles. I visited several societies, preached to the people, and came to Baltimore, in Maryland, the 27th of March, three hundred and twenty-two miles from Petersburg, the way I came; in my course through the Continent, since I left Baltimore the 11th of last April, it is about three thousand seven hundred and seven miles, in the sixty-sixth year of my age.

On March the 27th, Bishop Whatcoat arrived from his southern tour, at Baltimore, bringing to a close another year of his Episcopacy. He was now sixty-six years old, and had traveled about thirty-seven hundred miles in his new labors.

Bishop Asbury joined Bishop Whatcoat at Baltimore, in a conference on April 1, 1802. "Our conference began at Baltimore," says Bishop Whatcoat, "the 1st of April, and closed the 5th: four traveling, and five local preachers were ordained to the Deacon's office, and one to the Elder's office."

Immediately after the conference the two Bishops left for a tour to the eastern shore of Maryland, Virginia and Delaware. They continued on to Philadelphia and New York, holding conferences at each place. Bishop Whatcoat says of these conferences: "Here (Philadelphia) our conference began on the 1st of May, and closed the 6th; seven preachers were ordained to the Deacon's and three to the Elder's office; we visited the societies in New Jersey, and came to New York the 25th, 1802; about two hundred and four miles the way we took. Our Conference began at New York, the 1st of June, and closed the 5th; eleven traveling and three local preachers were ordained to the Deacon's, and seven to the Elder's offices."

They then set out to hold a conference on July the 1st, 1802, in Monmouth, Maine, this being the first conference to be held north of. Lynn, Massachusetts Bishop Whatcoat tells of this journey as follows:

The 7th, we pursued our course through the states of New York, Connecticut, Massachusetts, and New Hampshire, to Monmouth, in the county of Kennebec, in the District of Maine; here our Conference began the 1st of July, and closed the 3rd: we ordained four preachers to the Deacon's, and four to the Elder's office; the way we traveled from New York to Boston, was about three hundred and three miles, and from Boston to Monmouth, one hundred and seventy-three miles. We had a large gathering of people for this newly settled country, and a good prospect of the spread of religion.

At this point they separated and Bishop Whatcoat took a northwest course, crossing the northern part of New York, and continued along Lake Erie about one hundred miles. "Here Bishop Asbury," says Whatcoat, "and I parted for a few months; he passed through the country to hold Conference in Cumberland, in the state of Tennessee, the 1st of October, and I took a north-west course, through the notch of the mountain, by Dartmouth College, Mosischo Bay, Lake Champlain, Ballstown Springs, Cayuga Lake, Genessee, Buffalo, Cataraugus, Chateaugai, and so up the east side of Lake Erie, about one hundred miles; a rich soil, thinly settled, partly by the white people, and partly by Indians. I crossed the Ohio near Charlestown, and so passed on, partly an east and south-east course, through Redstone, Pennsylvania."

Bishop Whatcoat returned through Pennsylvania and Virginia to Georgetown, Delaware. This trip was a very dangerous one because they had traveled through the wilderness of the north-west inhabited by the Indians. They traveled about one thousand seven hundred and sixteen miles on this trip.

From this time until the next conference, Bishop Whatcoat's services were principally confined to the middle Atlantic states. During this time he says: "I attended several quarterly meetings, and ordained twelve local preachers to the Deacon's office; our congregations were large and solemn; at Winchester and Fairfax, the Lord was powerfully present to wound and to heal: I believe not less than twenty were converted at these two meetings.

"On the 21st of December, 1802, I took a circuit through Frederick, Rystertown, Baltimore, Annapolis, Federal City, Alexandria, Fredericksburg, Richmond, and Petersburg, so on to Edward Droomgoole's. Here our Conference began the 1st of March, and closed the 5th, in great peace. I ordained five traveling, and four local preachers to the Deacon's, and three to the Elder's office; Sabbath day was a great day: after the love-feast the public service continued from 11 o'clock, until 9 at night, in the woods: it was thought twenty, if not thirty, were converted; from Georgetown to Droomgoole's, the course I have taken, it is about four hundred and sixty-six miles: the 7th of March, I returned, and came to Baltimore, the 27th, two hundred and eighty-three miles from Droomgoole's."

On April 1, 1803, the conference met at Baltimore, and closed the 6th. Whatcoat says, "I ordained four

preachers to the Deacon's, and six to the Elder's office;
in the city and at the Point about seventy sermons were
preached, in the space of six days; strong exhortations
followed, and many were converted. In the last twelve
months I have traveled about three thousand seven
hundred and seven miles, and in the sixty-seventh year
of my age, though I have had considerable afflictions,
which have greatly shaken this house of clay."

After the conference adjourned, Bishop Asbury
joined Bishop Whatcoat on his trip through Delaware
to New York, holding several conferences. Bishop
Whatcoat says:

"The 11th of April, Bishop Asbury and I set out for
the east: we took a little circuit through Hartford,
Cecil, Kent, Queen Anne, Talbot, and Dorset circuits,
and returned to Duck Creek Cross Roads, in the state
of Delaware. Here our conference began May 2nd,
1803, and closed the 5th. I ordained twelve traveling
and five local preachers to the Deacon's, and twelve to
the Elder's office; we had a very large gathering of
preachers and people, and we were indulged with the
privilege of holding our conference in the Friends'
meeting-house; the 7th, we rode to Wilmington, and
the 10th, to Philadelphia, the way we traveled from
Baltimore, is about three hundred and fifty-two miles.
We left the city the 16th, and preached at Bristol and
Burlington; and came to New York the 19th, and after
settling some affairs, and the exercises of the Sabbath,
(though we had little rest that night, the alarm of fire
continuing a great part of the night, the bread fac-
tory being in flames) on the 23rd, we continued our
course through the White Plains, Bedford, Reading,
Stratford, New Haven, Middletown, Hebron, Wind-
ham, so on to Boston; the distance from Philadelphia

to Boston, is about three hundred and seventy-four miles."

Bishop Asbury was not well and Bishop Whatcoat's strength was growing weaker from the task of his office and age.

"May 27," says Asbury, "the Baptists of Connecticut have sent their petition from the Assembly to the Legislature of Connecticut to the bishops of the Methodist Church, that they may have their aid in obtaining toleration. What can we do, and how is it our business? We are neither popes nor politicians. Let our brethren assert their own liberties. Besides, who may now be trusted with power? The Baptists are avowed enemies to episcopacy, be the form of church government as mild as it may. Now it seems, popes, as they would otherwise term us, may be useful to them, nor are they too proud to ask for help; but our people will not be pushed into their measures; their bishops have no coercive power of this sort. If the Baptists know not what to do we cannot tell them." We would welcome the answer to this problem even today, although we do not support this attitude toward our Baptist friends. There may be a lot accomplished if we are willing to co-operate today.

The work was steadily growing in the east, making it more difficult and greater in enormity. They went on to Boston, where they held the New England conference. "Here," says Bishop Whatcoat, "our conference began on the 9th of June, and closed the 11th; one preacher was ordained to the Deacon's, and two to the Elder's office; the 12th of June, we turned our course to the west, through Waltham, Haverard, New Marlborough, Portland, Chesterfield, Brattleborough, Bennington, to Ashgrove or Cambridge, in the state of

Richard Whatcoat Monument erected by the Philadelphia Annual
Conference in 1855

New York, over a hilly, rocky, mountainous country, about one hundred and eighty miles from Boston."

The following account is taken from Bishop Asbury's Journal: "How can this city and Massachusetts be in any other than a melancholy state, worse, perhaps, for true piety than any other parts of the Union? What! reading priests, and alive? O, no, dead, dead, dead, by nature, by formality, by sin!"

After the conference adjourned, they continued in company visiting the societies in New England. On July 1, 1803, they held a conference at Ashgrove, New York. Asbury gives a fine description of this conference in the following:

"We opened our conference at John Baker's, in the Holloway, prettily environed with hills, a carpet of green spread beneath, and here and there around us fields clothed with the promise of an abundant harvest. We finished our business on Tuesday, public and private. There were nearly seventy preachers and fifty members. On the Sabbath day, perhaps, we had two thousand hearers: the house was filled with women, and the men stood without; I stood in the door, and spoke to them from 1 Tim. 4:11, 12; but I had been overcome by twelve hours' a day constant attention to business in the conference, and spoke with pain."

Bishop Whatcoat adds that fifteen traveling and two local preachers were ordained to the Deacon's orders, and five to the Elder's office at this conference. On July 6, Asbury makes note of the following event: "We came to Pittstown, dined with Mr. Follitt, and came on to the Half Moon, thirty miles, and lodged at John Barber's. On Thursday we came through Albany, and stopped to dine at Dole's tavern, three miles beyond. Here Brother Whatcoat discovered that he had left my coat and my cloak behind. I bore the loss with some patience. Finding we had two hundred miles to reach Trenton and only six days to accomplish the distance in, we continued on to Goeyman's Landing. Reflecting on this, and the journey of fourteen hundred miles still to Kentucky, and Brother Whatcoat's indisposition withal, I felt somewhat moved. On Friday we came to John Crawford's, near the Catskill Mountains, making thirty-five miles without food for man or beast. On Saturday we reached Cole's, at Hurley, on Esopus Creek. The drought and heat and dust. in nine hundred and ninety miles from Baltimore to this place, made us suffer, but my mind was supported, and my health preserved."

They, then, returned by way of Trenton, and finally to Philadelphia. Here Bishop Whatcoat was once again visited with his old infirmities of body from which he had suffered for many years. After a few days of rest, he journeyed on until he had to lay aside his work until the General Conference of 1804.

When the General Conference opened in Baltimore on May 7, 1804, it found Bishop Whatcoat once more ready for active service. This conference, being the fourth General Conference, was composed of one hundred and seven members, representing the whole Methodist Episcopal Church of America. The conference was in session seventeen days. Again we see Bishop Coke's name appear on the roll along with Bishop Asbury and Bishop Whatcoat.

Bishop Coke presided, as he was the senior bishop. Bishop Asbury says, "Our General Conference began. What was done, the revised Form of Discipline will show. There were attempts made upon the ruling eldership. We had a great talk. I talked little upon any subject. I preached but twice.

"The Lord did not own the ministerial labors of the General Conference. It was a doubt if any souls were converted. I prayed for hundreds, but God did not answer my prayer."

The "Book Concern" was ordered removed from Philadelphia, to New York. It was at this conference that Methodism deliberately, and in its Constitutional law, by vote, declared the republic of the United States was no longer a Confederacy, but a Nation, and as such supreme and sovereign over all its states. Likewise, the subject of Slavery was, as usual, debated. Bishop Whatcoat says, "I sat with them ten days, but the inflammation in my eyes was so violent that I was obliged to withdraw; but my kind Doctor Wilkins gave me a poultice which checked the violence of the tumor. On the 23rd. our conference closed in great peace and much love."

At the close of the conference Bishop Whatcoat set out for the west on July 17, 1804. He was forced to travel with less rapidity and more caution due to his failing strength. At the home of Harry Stevens in the latter part of September, he found Bishop Asbury confined to his bed with a severe fever. He remained with Bishop Asbury a month; until he had recuperated sufficiently to travel. They started on their westward trip, but had gone less than a hundred miles when the fever returned, and Bishop Whatcoat, leaving Bishop Asbury, was compelled to travel alone through the western wilderness, with little money and provisions. He passed through Wheeling, West Virginia, crossing the Ohio River and continued his way up the Muskingum and Hockhocking rivers, visiting all the young societies along the way. He again crossed the

Ohio River into Kentucky, where he was to have held the western conference on October 2nd at Mount Gerizim, but it was now the first of November. He visited all the societies, encouraging them and their preachers in their work. Then, he began to turn his face eastward, through Tennessee into South Carolina, where he held a conference, at Charleston, on January 1, 1805. Bishop Whatcoat says that he ordained one to the Deacon's office and four to the Elder's office.

Bishop Asbury again joined him here before the conference had adjourned. They started north from Charleston, holding conferences in North Carolina and Virginia, and on to Baltimore. While crossing the Tar River, the boat in which they were filled with water, yet, they arrived safely at the shore. At a conference in Charleston, on January 1, 1805, Bishop Asbury notes in review of Methodism in the West and South says: "We have admitted upon trial, eighteen preachers in the Western, and eleven in the Southern conferences; and added two thousand members within the bounds of each, notwithstanding a great morality, and the constant removal to new lands."

They held the Philadelphia Conference at Chestertown, Maryland, on May 1st, 1805. Bishop Whatcoat mentions that they ordained three Deacons, and two Elders. Among these, Bishop Asbury gives the name of Boehm being ordained an Elder. This is significant because Henry Boehm became Bishop Asbury's traveling companion and later historian of Early Methodism.

On the adjournment of the conference, they departed for New York. They stopped at Philadelphia, where they learned that Sarah Williams, at her death, left 200 pounds to the disposal of Bishop Whatcoat and Bishop Asbury. They immediately ordered its application to the Chartered Fund.

The New York Conference was held at a camp meeting at Stillwater, near Ashgrove, New York. Bishop Whatcoat says: "On Friday, the 7th of June, our camp meeting began at a place called Stillwater; about twenty tents were erected, and about five hundred people attended. In the night rain descended, but our meeting continued about thirty hours, notwithstanding the rain. Many continued in singing, prayer, and exhortation, with little intermission. On Saturday, there were about forty tents. On the Sabbath it was thought that five or six thousand people attended, and about sixty preachers. Monday, about five o'clock in the evening we closed our meeting. A considerable number were brought under the powerful operations of grace."

On June 12, 1805, they opened the conference at Ashgrove, Cambridge County, New York. They ordained seven Deacons and nine Elders. At the close of the conference, the Bishops parted again, Bishop Asbury going to the east and Bishop Whatcoat to the west. This conference closed his fifth year in the Episcopal office. He was again to visit the frontier societies before being called to his final resting place. Bishop Whatcoat on his western tour, visited a few days with Freeborn Garrettson.

Bishop Asbury joined Bishop Whatcoat and they returned to Baltimore on March 8, 1806. During all this final tour, Bishop Whatcoat was growing weaker and suffering severely; but he would not fail to fulfill his duties to the church to which God had called him.

The Baltimore Conference met on March 14, 1806, and the harvest field seemed to be ripe for garnering. Many souls were saved as there had been almost everywhere he had gone. This was to be the last conference that he would attend before the great summons of death. In order that we may understand the heavy strain through which he was going, we quote the following:

"Notwithstanding my infirm state of body, through the blessing of God, I have been able to travel three thousand four hundred and sixteen miles the last twelve months, stopping one-fourth of the time at different places by the way.

"July 22nd, I continued my course through Carlisle, Shippensburgh, Bedford, Berlin, Canals Town, Union Town, Washington, West Liberty, and crossed the Ohio near Weeland; and have great reason to bless God, who has preserved me these many years as an itinerant preacher, during which time he hath delivered me from many afflictions of body and mind."

At the close of the conference, the Bishops parted to labor in their respective fields. Bishop Whatcoat went to the eastern shore of Maryland and Delaware, on his way to Philadelphia to attend the conference that would convene on the 14th of April. His health was now rapidly failing him, and his pace was slackened by the long road over which he had journeyed. His last sermon this side of the Great Divide he preached in Milford, Delaware, on the 8th of April. The next day, Bishop Asbury and his companion overtook him on the way. Bishop Whatcoat was taken into Bishop Asbury's carriage. On the way, he was taken very ill, and it was feared by his companions that he would die immediately. They were able to make Dover, Delaware, where they were forced to leave him at the home of an old friend, Governor Richard Bassett. Here he was given all the care and treatment that mortal hands and hearts of friends were capable of performing.

Bishop Asbury was forced to go to Philadelphia, to preside over the conference. This was a sad farewell between the two who had served as "laborers together with God" for twenty-two years in the American wilderness to lead the weary and sinful souls back to God. To these two men, Methodism in America owes most for their untiring labors and devotion.

Bishop Whatcoat lingered for thirteen weeks, suffering unknown pain, yet receiving it with all cheerfulness, "for by suffering we are made perfect." This he proved by the calm and placid way which he met the monster death and triumphantly conquered the foe that had so troubled him in his youth. On the fifth of July, 1806, Richard Whatcoat slipped away to be with Christ. His earthly remains were laid to rest beneath the altar of Wesley Chapel, Dover, Delaware.

The old Wesley Chapel was removed in 1850, and renamed Whatcoat Methodist Episcopal Church, which is used by the negro congregation of Dover. In the vestibule of the new Wesley Church there is to be found the marble slab inserted within the wall, bearing his memorial. Upon his grave now stands a large and beautiful monument erected in 1855 by the Philadelphia Annual Conference at the consecration of Wesley Church. A part of the inscription reads as follows: "This stone marks the site of the old Wesley Church erected in 1780. The grave being under the pulpit." It further states in testimony to his life: "In life and in death, he was the model of a Christian, a minister, and a scriptural bishop." The part omitted here is the historical part of his life which has been given elsewhere.

The whole Methodist Church paid particular respect to his memory. Several annual conferences at their sessions following his death, requested Bishop Asbury to preach his funeral sermon. This he did with all solemnity of the occasion.

At Dover, the place of Bishop Whatcoat's death, March 30, 1807, Bishop Asbury preached his funeral sermon from 2 Timothy 3:10: "But thou hast fully known my doctrine, manner of life, purpose, faith, long-suffering, charity, patience."

Richard Whatcoat and Francis Asbury had known each other before coming to America. Bishop Asbury stated that he was fourteen years old when he first met Richard Whatcoat, who was eight years his senior.

From Bishop Asbury's Journal was given this quotation: "On my return to Philadelphia, I found a letter from Dr. Chandler, declaring the death of Bishop Whatcoat, that father in Israel, and my faithful friend for forty years—a man of solid parts, a self-denying man of God. Who ever heard him speak an idle word? When was guile found in his mouth? He had been thirty-eight years in the ministry—sixteen years in England, Wales, and Ireland, and twenty-two years in America; twelve years as presiding elder, four of this time he was stationed in the cities or traveling with me, and six years in the superintendency. A man so uniformly good I have not known in Europe or America. He had long been afflicted with gravel and stone, in which afflictions, nevertheless, he traveled a great deal—three thousand miles the last year: he bore in the last three months excessively painful illness with most exemplary patience." Bishop Asbury changed his route in order to visit him, but "death," says he, "was too quick for me."

"Like a sick child that knoweth not his mother while
    she blesses,
And drops upon his burning brow the coolness of her
    kisses;
That turns his fevered eyes around—
My Mother! Where's my Mother?
As if such tender words and looks could come from
    any other!
The fever gone, with leaps of heart he sees her bend-
    ing o'er him,
Her face all pale from watchful love, the unweary love
    she bore him!
Thus woke the Poet from the dream his life's long
    fever gave him,
Beneath those deep pathetic eyes which closed in
death to save him.

Thus? oh, not thus! no type of earth could image that
    awaking,
Wherein he scarcely heard the chant of seraphs round
    him breaking,
Or felt the new immortal throb of soul from body
    parted,
But felt those eyes alone, and knew
My Saviour! not deserted!"

CHAPTER XIII.

THE PREACHER.

It may do us all some good, even at this late day, to seek a closer acquaintance with "this serene, gentle, and holy man who was sent to the young American Church, as if for a sample, to show what a life of peace and holiness a Christian may attain on earth, where sincerity, privation, diligence, watchfulness, love of divine communion, and humble, and active faith do center."

"From the time of his entrance upon his work as an itinerant superintendent of the Methodist Episcopal Church," says Nathan Bangs, "until he was disabled by sickness and debility, he traveled regularly through his vast diocese, which extended over the entire continent, preaching almost every day to the people, visiting the annual conferences, sometimes in company with his venerable colleague, Bishop Asbury, and sometimes alone, discharging his responsible duties with marked satisfaction to all concerned. A complication of painful diseases arrested his career of usefulness, and compelled him to remit those public labors in which his soul had so long delighted. For thirteen weeks he bore with the most exemplary patience, and devout resignation to the divine will, the excruciating pains with which his body was afflicted, expressing, in the midst of them all, his faith in Christ and his firm hope of everlasting life, and finally triumphed over the 'last enemy,' being 'more than a conqueror through Him who loved him.'"

There is no better qualified authority on the character and life of Whatcoat than Bishop Asbury, for he says, "I have known Richard Whatcoat from the time

I was fourteen years of age to sixty-two years, most intimately, and have tried him most accurately in respect to the soundness of his faith, on the doctrines of human depravity, the complete and general atonement of Jesus Christ, the insufficiency of either moral or ceremonial righteousness for justification, in opposition to faith alone in the merit and righteousness of Christ, and the doctrine of regeneration and sanctification. I have also known his manner of life, at all times and places, before the people, both as a Christian and a minister; his long-suffering, for he was a man of great affliction, both of body and mind, having been exercised with severe diseases and great labor." The outstanding characteristic of Bishop Whatcoat was his Christian life. It was this characteristic that made him a soul-stirring preacher. Without a doubt, Bishop Whatcoat had lived for God alone, and had consecrated all his time and powers to the service of God and His Church. Therefore, he had neither time nor desire to "Lay up for himself, treasures upon earth, where moth and rust doth corrupt, and where thieves break through and steal," but his soul and heart were centered upon laying up for himself "treasures in heaven, where neither moth nor rust doth corrupt, and where thieves do not break through nor steal."

Thus, he died without possessions enough to defray the expense of his funeral. He was able to say to the world, as did Peter to the lame man. "Silver and gold have I none, but such as I have, give I thee." His life he gladly gave for others. and in the giving he was given.

Bishop Whatcoat was a great preacher because he had a great theme. Dr. Wakely says, "Holiness was his theme." Dr. Boehm states, "I have seen congregations melted under his appeals, like wax before the fire. His manner was mixed with mildness, energy, and power. He was a man of good principles, and personal magnetism. He died in my circuit in 1806."

Bishop Whatcoat's greatest sermons were preached by his character. "His beautiful character preached more effectually than his sermons. Peculiarly simple, sober, but serene and cheerful, living as well as teaching his favorite doctrine of sanctification, extremely prudent in his administration, pathetically impressive in discourse, and 'made perfect through sufferngs,' he is pre-eminently the saint in the primitive calendar of American Methodism."

His preaching was attended with a remarkable unction from on High. Bangs says, "Hence those who sat under his word, if they were believers in Christ, felt that it was good to be there, for his doctrine distilled as the dew upon the tender herb, and as the rain upon the mown grass. One who had heard him remarked, that though he could not follow him in all his researches—intimating that he went beyond his depth in some of his thoughts—yet he felt that he was listening to a messenger of God, not only from the solemnity of his manner, but also from the 'refreshing from the presence of the Lord,' which so manifestly accompanied his word. The softness of his persuasions won upon the affections of the heart, while the rich flow of gospel truth which dropped from his lips, enlightened the understanding."

His sermons bore a great likeness to those of the Reformers of the Seventeenth Century. The following is a sermon which he preached in John Street Church, New York:

Subject: On the Love of our Neighbor.

Text: "Thou shalt love thy neighbor as thyself."
Rom. 13:9.

The holy apostle having proved at large that Jew
and Gentile had sinned, and come short of the glory of
God; and that there was but one way for their recov-
ery, which was through the redemption which is in
Christ Jesus, admonishes Christians, in the twelfth
and following chapters, to several relative duties. One
which he strongly enforces is, "to obey the Civil Powers, not only through fear, but for conscience' sake;
for there is no power but of God; the powers that be,
are ordained of God: "the power is of God; the abuse
of it is of man.   After speaking of several branches of
the Christian duty, he ads, "if there be any other com-
mandment, it is summed up in this saying, 'Thou shalt
love thy neighbor as thyself.' "   But "who is my neighbor?"   Perhaps there is a nearer relation subsisting
among men than most people are aware of.   Is not
God the "Father of the Spirits of all flesh?" hath he
not "made of one blood all nations dwelling on the face
of the earth?"   If we have one father; are of one
blood, one family; are all his offspring, and are "the
sheep of his pasture," then all men are neighbors.   If
any distinction is to be made, it is in the case of him
that acts the neighborly part of showing mercy. (Luke
10:31).

But what is our duty to our neighbor?   Thou shalt
love thy neighbor as thyself.   Love is the essence of
religion—the bond and perfection of every duty we
owe to God, and our neighbor; therefore "love is the
fulfilling of the law."   But this embraces the disposi-
tion and temper of the mind and heart,—the words
of our lips and the actions of our lives.   St. Peter admonishes us also to love one another, with a pure

heart fervently (1 Peter 1:22). Paul adds, "Be ye kind one to another, tender-hearted, forgiving one another, even as God, for Christ's sake, hath forgiven you." (Eph. 4:32). St. John says, "Beloved, let us love one another; for love is of God." (John 4:9). "God is love: and he that dwelleth in love, dwelleth in God, and God in him," (4:16) ; and our Lord adds, "I say unto you, love your enemies." (Matt. 5:44). What a heavenly temper is this!

> Soft peace she brings, wherever she arrives;
> She builds our quiet, reforms our lives;
> Lays the rough paths of peevish nature even,
> And opens in each heart a little heaven.

But, secondly, loving words, as St. Paul advises, speaking the truth in love. (Eph. 4:15). Let no corrupt communication proceed out of your mouth; but that which is good to the use of edifying, that it may minister grace unto the hearers." (29). "Let your speech be alway with grace, seasoned with salt, that ye may know how ye ought to answer every man." (Col. 4:6). "For our conversation is in heaven; from whence we look for the Saviour, the Lord Jesus Christ, who shall change our vile body, that it may be fashioned like unto his glorious body, (Phil. 3:20, 21) ; and the Apostle James adds, "Who is a wise man, and endued with knowledge among you let him show out of a good conversation, his works with meekness of wisdom," (St. James 3:13) ; and our Lord says, "Let your communication be yea, yea, nay, nay, for whatsoever is more than these cometh of evil."

But thirdly, loving actions give lustre to, and are the growing fruit of a true faith and a loving heart; agreeable to what the beloved disciple saith, "Whoso hath the world's goods, and seeth his brother have need, and shutteth up his bowels of compassion from him, how dwelleth the love of God in him? My little children, let us love in deed and in truth," (1 John 3:17, 18) ; and again, "Blessed are they that do his commandments, that they may have right to the tree of life, and may enter in through the gates into the city." (Rev. 22:14). Also the wise master-builder saith "Be not deceived; God is not mocked; for whatsoever a man soweth, that shall the also reap, (Gal. 6:7) ; for he that soweth to the flesh, shall of the flesh reap corruption; but he that soweth to the Spirit, shall of the Spirit reap life everlasting." "As we have, therefore, opportunity, let us do good unto all men, especially unto them that are of the household of faith." (Chap. 6:8, 10). How beautiful does our Lord set his seal to this doctrine, when he says unto them on his right hand, "Come, ye blessed of my Father, inherit the kingdom prepared for you from the foundation of the world: for I was an hungered, and ye gave me meat: I was thirsty, and ye gave me drink: I was a stranger, and ye took me in: naked, and ye clothed me: I was sick, and ye visited me: I was in prison, and ye came unto me," (Matt. 25:34, 35, 36, 46) ; these shall go into life eternal. The duty is plain; but in what sense are we to "Love our neighbors as ourselves?"—are we to feel equal warmth of affection to all men; are we to use the same freedom of speech and perform towards all the same acts of love? Must we make every one equal sharers of the comforts and blessings which we enjoy? This cannot be consistent with the dispensations of Providence. The relative duties of husbands and wives, parents and children, masters and servants, rulers and subjects, ministers and people, demand particular attention; to relative duties besides obligations particular people may impose upon themselves; such as promises, vows, and covenants: as the case of Jonathan and David, or persons traveling to a far country, agreeing to share in each other's prosperity and adversity. In these and various other cases, a particular attention must be paid to the relative stations of different persons. How, then, shall we judge of our love to our neighbor? I confess I know no better rule, than what our Lord imposed, namely, "Whatsoever ye would men should do to you, do ye even so to them; for this is the law and the prophets." (Matt. 7:12). In all difficult cases, suppose yourself in their situation, and them in yours; and how you would wish they should act towards you, do ye so towards them.

But why must we love our neighbors as ourselves? Because God commands us so to do. "Thou shalt love thy neighbor as thyself." (See Lev. 19:18; Matt. 22:39; Gal. 5:14; James 2:8). But our happiness and usefulness in time, as well as our felicity in eternity, depend much on the performance of this duty. The spirit of love is the most happy temper we can possess; it sweetens all our labor, and makes "our willing feet in swift obedience move." The devils believe, and tremble too; but they cannot love: this is a cordial and support under all our burdens and sufferings in life; and it will not leave us at death.

Seeing then that our happiness and usefulness, in time and eternity, so much depend on this duty; let us inquire, how we may acquire this spirit and practice.

Consider this duty in all its branches, how reasonable, how profitable it is! how does it advance the dignity of man! But remember, that the love of our neighbor springs from the "love of God shed abroad

The House of Governor Richard Bassett, Dover, Delaware, where Whatcoat remained during his illness, and departing from this life on July 5, 1806

in our hearts by the Holy Ghost given unto us." He that loveth God, loveth his brother also. (1 John 4:21). That you may not come short of this privilege, seek it with your whole heart; in the use of all the means of grace; in private and family, as well as public prayer; hearing the word of God read, or expounded; in the Sacrament, striving to discern the Lord's body: attending to every branch of domestic and social duty; be fervent and constant in meditation and self-examination; denying yourselves all ungodliness, and taking up your cross daily. That you may be profited by these means of grace, let no sin be indulged,—"bring them all out, and let them be slain before the Lord:" "cease to do evil, learn to do well;" "call to remembrance all the sins you have committed by thought, word, or deed, against God, your neighbor, or your own soul; think what you have caused the Lord Jesus Christ to suffer, that he might redeem your soul from sin, death, and hell; how much your neighbor has been injured by your guilt, and to what you have exposed your own soul! how many duties you have neglected,—how much your heart has been set on things temporal, and how little on things eternal." "Consider how short and uncertain life is! how soon death will overtake us! how awful it is to appear before the judgment seat of Christ unprepared!—weep and mourn over your past transgressions and your present miseries." Consider the purity of God's holy law, how it extends to the thoughts and intents of the heart, and how it curses every one "that continues not in all things which are written in the book of the law to do them;" remember how unable you are to make your own heart clean, or to atone for one sin; confess your guilt and helplessness; and lay yourself before the throne of mercy, be-

seeching Almighty God to forgive your manifold transgressions, for the sake of Jesus Christ, your great High
Priest. As delays are dangerous, come now; as you
cannot grow better by living at a distance from God,
come just as you are; believe that God is willing to forgive you all that is past! Plead the merits of Christ's
death as he "died for your sins, and rose again for your
justification; the just for the unjust, that he might
bring you to God;" wait at the door of mercy, till the
Lord, whom ye seek, "shall suddenly come to his tem-
ple;" till the love of God is shed abroad in your heart
by the Holy Ghost given unto you,—thus will you find
"wisdom's ways to be ways of pleasantness, and all
her paths paths of peace," and so you will triumph
over the sinful course, and spirit of the wicked world;
then it will be your "meat and drink to do the will of
your Father, who is in heaven." That you may not
come short of your duty and highest privilege, pray
"that God would sanctify you wholly; and that your
whole spirit, and soul, and body may be preserved
blameless, unto the coming of our Lord Jesus Christ,
knowing that faithful is he that calleth you, who also
will do it."

Now behold this holy train of heaven-born, heaven-
bound souls how they rise into glory. As they run
their steady course like the sun, that enlightens the
world, and enlivens all nature, so, likewise, these send
forth their enlightening rays, and the moral world is
enlightened by the brightness thereof; the wicked are
convinced: mourners are encouraged, and the way of
life guarded. Their spirit, like the sun, breathes life
into all around, while thousands emerge from darkness
and death; and the generations to come shall rise to
praise the Lord, who shall be as diadems in their

crowns of rejoicing, in that day when the Bridegroom
of the Church shall appear and say, "Well done, good
and faithful servants, enter ye into the joy of your
Lord!" O, what sweetness of spirit do they enjoy, what
peace of conscience, what heavenly transports, what
communion with God, what fellowship with the excellent ones of the earth! See how meek, how gentle,
how patient, how resigned they are under every dispensation of Providence! how steadfast in faith!
Though the earth stagger like a drunken man; though
the hills be removed, and the mountains cast into the
depth of the sea, yet will they not fear; though they
walk through the valley of the shadow of death; yet
will they fear no evil, for thou art with them; thy
rod and thy staff will comfort them; could you see
them in their closets,—how fervent in spirit, how open
to conviction, how willing to acknowledge their sins
and imperfections before the Lord, how ready to
amend what appears to be wrong! What little dependence in their works of righteousness! what an entire
dependence on the great atonement of Christ; how
honest in their dealings! how faithful to their promises; how upright in their walk! how heavenly in their
conversations! what respect for the word, house. and
ordinances of God! how strict in keeping the Lord's
day!

"These are they which follow the Lamb whither-
soever he goeth," who are blessed in life, supported
in death, confessed, acquitted, owned, and rewarded in
the tremendous Day of Judgment! And could you follow
them to the regions of glory, and see them invested in
their blood-washed linen; when the world, sin, death,
hell, and the devil are finally overcome, O what amaz-
ing discoveries will open to their view! what displays

of redeeming love will be unfolded! from what depths
of woe will they be raised; what dangers have they
escaped! what straits and difficult paths have they
been brought through! and now the full glory of the
Lamb adorns the heavenly plain,—O what bursting
joys will swell their enraptured souls! O what companies, what pleasures, what harmony, what sounds of
praise! Hear how they echo, and then eternal wonders
open in infinite succession:—but where shall my growing wonders end?—it is enough. "Eye hath not seen,
ear hath not heard, nor hath it entered into the heart
of man to conceive what God hath prepared for them
that love him."

But art thou the person? Dost thou love thy neighbor as thyself? Is "the love of God shed abroad in thy
heart, by the Holy Ghost given unto thee?" Do loving
tempers, words, and actions, witness to all about thee,
that thou art heaven-born and heaven-bound? Has no
"sin dominion over thee?" Art thou meek, patient,
and resigned? Hast thou communion with God, and
fellowship with the saints? Canst thou trust God with
all thy concerns? Canst thou claim all the promises
of the Gospel, as "yea and amen," to thy believing
soul? If so, "walk by the same rule;" lose no opportunity of doing good according to thy power; the harvest will come; "be thou faithful unto death," always
abounding in the work of the Lord, forasmuch as our
labor in the Lord is not in vain.

And now, I address myself to various classes of
people; and, first, a word to the wicked. O, wicked
man, see from what heights of glory thou hast fallen!
Art thou destitute of the love of God and thy neighbor?
What is the opposite temper? Is there any medium?
Canst thou lie neutral in this war? - Say then, art

thou a hater of God and thy neighbor? What fellowship canst thou have in his company, while thy passions rage with fury, like Cain's, ready to consume thy
nearest friends, and rebel against thy God? Thy
words are stout against God; and are used to flatter,
deceive, or defame thy brother. Thy "feet are swift to
shed blood," and tread the broad frequented way that
leads to death ;thy hands are open to catch the prey, and
leave the widow and fatherless in deep distress; thy
eyes are roving to the ends of the earth after vanity;
thy ears are open to the charms of the world. O vain
man! how long wilt thou grasp at shadows? how long
wilt thou seek death in the error of thy ways? how
wilt thou feel when death lays his cold hands upon
thee, and thy blood chills in thy veins? To which of
thy companions wilt thou turn? where are all thy
comforters fled? But if this is grievous for thee to
hear, how wilt thou stand the shock when Gabriel's
trumpet wakes the dead, and "small and great stand"
before the inexorable Judge? Will thy ears be
charmed, or thy eyes ravished with the sight, "when
the books are opened," and "thou art weighed in the
balances?" Canst thou bear the thought of being
driven to eternal darkness? Art thou willing to reap
the wages of sin? O look, look well before thou
plungest into that abyss of woe! See what a gulf lies
between Dives and Lazarus! O eternity! if thou canst
not bear eternal torments, lay down the weapons of
thy rebellion; repent of thy sin, and folly, and "seek
the Lord while he may be found; call upon him while
he is near;" and so iniquity shall not prove thy ruin.

But a word to formal professors. You "thank God
that you are not as other men, nor even as this pub-
lican;" you have no pleasure in drinking, dancing,

gaming, cheating, sabbath-breaking, swearing, lying, quarrelling, revenge, etc. You delight to read your Bible; say many prayers; attend sermons, and sacrament; can tell what it costs you to support the Church and poor yearly; and, perhaps, you are not afraid to dispute with any man upon any article of your faith. So far it may be well. But will you substitute this for "Loving our neighbors as ourselves?" Know ye not, that "if you speak with the tongues of men and angels, and have not love, you are become as sounding brass, or a tinkling cymbal; and though you have the gift of prophecy, and understand all mysteries, and all knowledge: and though you have all faith, so that you could remove mountains, and have not love, you are nothing; and though you bestow all your goods to feed the poor, and though you give your body to be burned, and have not love, it profiteth you nothing." O, formal professor! delay not with the foolish virgins; but bring thy filthy garments to "the blood of sprinkling, and wash in the laver of regeneration," and trust in him who has said, "except I wash thee, thou hast no part in me." Lay thy works, thy sins, and thy soul at Jesus' feet; plead the merit of his death for thy justification; rely upon the purifying operation of the Holy Ghost for thy sanctification, and the graces and the fruit of the Spirit for thy inward and outward adornment; then wilt thou say with the poet,

> Bold shall I stand in thy great day,
> For who aught to my charge shall lay?
> Jesus, thy blood and righteousness,
> My beauty, are my glorious dress:
> 'Midst flaming worlds, in these arrayed,
> With joy shall I lift up my head.

But a word to the backslider,—whether in heart, lip, or life. Remember "from whence thou art fallen;" thou hast turned thy back upon the vanities of a wicked world, with its sinful customs and practices; thou hast felt the horrors of a guilty conscience, and hast experienced the pangs of the new birth; thou "hast tasted of the good word of God, and the powers of the world to come, and hast been a partaker of the Holy Ghost;" thou wast happy in God; a light in a benighted world, and bid fair for eternal life; but how is it now? Is thy fine gold become dim? Hast thou lost thy first love? Is the throne of grace as brass to thy prayers? Are thy comforts fled? Has thy beloved withdrawn the smiles of his reconciled countenance? Hast thou lost sight of glory? Hast thou let in the spirit of the world? Art thou seeking comfort in the company, pleasures, riches, or honors of this world? Will these satisfy thy immortal soul? O stop, and view what awaits apostatizing spirits! Canst thou bear the vengeance of eternal fire to be poured out on thy apostate soul in one eternal storm? If not, turn again unto him from whom thou hast so deeply revolted! But art thou ready to say, 'there is not hope. it is too late; I have sinned against light; God will no more be entreated by such a rebel as me; I fear that I have committed the unpardonable sin; and that my sin is unto death.' Well, poor soul, thou canst but be lost! But how dost thou know what God will do for thee? Canst thou measure the depth of divine mercy? Dost thou know the virtue of that blood that cleanses from all sin? Canst thou tell how far the all-prevailing merits and mediation of our great High Priest may extend towards thee? Oh, make trial once more; enter into covenant with the God of thy salvation, that if

184 LIFE OF BISHOP RICHARD WHATCOAT

"he will heal thy backslidings, thou wilt love him with all thy heart, and serve him with all thy strength." Use the form and seek the power of godliness; take courage, plead the promises; and "be not faithless, but believing." "The Lord is longsuffering, not willing that any should perish;" plead the mercy of God. Thou art out of hell! if thou art a condemned sinner, yet thou art not a damned ghost; if sunk into sin, thou art not shut up in the bottomless abyss of unquenchable fire! yet the door of mercy is open. "While thou hast breath, call upon the name of the Lord;" why should a living man complain? how much better is thy state than that of the rich man on the other side of the gulf? Only "acknowledge thy backslidings, and turn unto me, saith the Lord, and I will heal thy backslidings and love thee freely!" (Hosea 14:5). "If any man sin, we have an advocate with the Father, Jesus Christ the Righteous; and he is the propitiation for our sins, and not for ours only, but also for the sins of the whole world." "Behold the Lamb of God, that taketh away the sins of the world!" See him pleading thy cause before the throne of love.

> The Father hears him pray;
> His dear anointed one;
> He cannot turn away
> The presence of his Son;
> The Spirit answers to the blood,
> And tells me I am born of God.

And now I commend you to God, and to the word of his grace, who is able to build you up, and to give you an inheritance among them that are sanctified. Now unto him that is able to do exceeding abundantly above all that we ask or think, according to the power that worketh in us; unto him be glory in the

Church, by Jesus Christ, throughout all ages, world without end! Amen.

A poem found among Mr. Whatcoat's writings:

Fair Salem, the seat of I AM; the region where
    pleasures do grow,
The grove where contentment doth reign,
Where transports forever do flow;
When shall I remove to thy joys,
When shall I behold them in full?
Thy glories my bosom do warm!
All earth is but heavy and dull.

When, Jesus, will sighs be all over?
When shall I to earth bid adieu?
When shall I 'midst angels rise?
And all thy bright ravishments view?
See how I'm encompassed about
With trouble, temptations, and woe;
Mark how I my banishment mourn,
And how I mourn home for to go.

This region's insipid and dry,
There's nothing my joys to increase;
My craving all centered in God.
And only in him have I peace.
I burn with contempt for the world,
I spurn all its pleasure and store;
While God, and his ways, and his word
I choose to be mine evermore.

O could I this moment depart,
And with my Redeemer arise
From earth and its sorrows, my heart
Forever with angels shall live,
The fields of ambrosia to walk.
These plains of ineffable sweets,
The streams of salvation to drink,
And shout as I pass through thy streets.

Bishop Whatcoat was a great lover of truth and righteousness in his own practice, and a great presser of them on his hearers, especially upon religious professors, exhorting them to be just in all their doings, true in their words, cautious in promising, and punctual in performing; he sharply reproved promise-breakers and deceitful dealing.

He was anxious for the conversion of sinners, and for the success of the Gospel. To promote this end he poured out his soul in prayer and preaching. "He imparted not only the word, but himself, as it were, to his hearers. His supplications and exhortations were so affectionate, so full of holy zeal and power, as to greatly move his auditors, and melt his congregation into tears and penetential sorrow, not by vain repetitions, crude expressions, unintelligible sense, or mysterious nonsense in place of prayer. His spirit was serious—his gesture reverent—his words well suited, well weighed, pithy, solid, and truly expressive of his truly humble and fervent desire after the things he asked. He was nigh to God, as become a creature overawed by the Majesty of his Creator. He prayed with the spirit and understanding, with faith, fervency, and humble importunity—his affections working, but rationally as well as strongly; by which he prevailed with his Redeemer, and on his hearers; because they found it to be exactly the habitual and constant frame of his mind; for he was always composed, serious, and grave. He set God always before him; and, wherever he was, he laboured to walk as in his presence." His main object in all things was to study to "show himself approved of God, the Father, who seeth in secret and rewardeth openly!" and "to keep a conscience void of offence in private devotion and converse with Christ and his own soul, delighting in secret prayer and retirement, when opportunity offered, that he might freely use his voice to his heavenly Father."

"My first journey with him," says Phoebus, "was over the Allegheny Mountains to the frontiers of Maryland, Pennsylvania, and Virginia. I found him so fixed in the ways of God, that nothing could disengage him, or move his patience, so as to make him mumur in the least degree. He was not wearied with fatigue or riding, or of preaching, so as to make him abate his private devotions; but after lecturing and praying several times a day in public, on retiring, he poured out his soul before he laid his body to rest; by which means he was ever ready to sound forth the high praises of his gracious Redeemer, at all times and on all occasions. His tours through the back woods were very dangerous; the Indians were not then at peace with the United States, but remained hostile, and made frequent incursions, and destroyed many families as well as single persons, whenever they met them; so that, some whom he preached to and baptized, in those parts, were killed and scalped a few weeks after. I think not less than seventy were miserably mangled and killed within one year and a half, in and about their own houses.

"Mr. Whatcoat appeared to be the same at all times, and under all circumstances;—to be as calm in the wilds as in the cultivated fields—in the smoky cabin as in the carpeted parlour—amidst the clamours of untoward children, where he was detained during the mountain storm, or flood of rain, that had raised the rivers so that they could not be forded.

"His voluntary labours and travels in America proved his strong attachment to the Redeemer's worldly gain, and worldly pleasure, which were strewed at his feet. He refused all, and preferred feeding the lambs of Jesus Christ, and calling sinners to repentance, to all the glories of the world. Forasmuch as the people who wished to be saved by hearing were scattered thinly through the country, to supply them with the word of life required a man to labour and travel in summer's sun and winter's frost, so that the people might not perish for lack of knowledge. Wearing himself out to give light and heat unto others, he allowed himself little rest; he rose at five in the morning, wherever he was, even in winter, that (first having communed with his Sovereign) he might be early at his studies, and well prepared to declare the accepted time of the Lord, and the day of salvation. His moderation was known to all who knew him. In all things he showed himself a pattern in piety, in doctrine, and zeal, —yet not rigid in his principles. He held that separation was sometimes necessary from known corruptions in church or state; but allowed no separation from a church, except compliance with some evil was made the condition of membership."

Richard Whatcoat was the possessor of high mental qualities which prepared him for a useful life of service, having been with Jesus and learned of him and from him to be meek and humble in heart. Phoebus says, "He appeared to enjoy the abiding witness of the Holy Spirit, and that rest to his soul promised by Jesus Christ, which he so pressingly recommended to others, by precept as well as example."

Bishop Whatcoat was a man whose judgment and opinions could be trusted, and his counsel was sought on important matters which concerned the Church. Such counselors and Saints were needed at that time as well as all time. Bishop Whatcoat was a living likeness of all that he taught others. "To sinners he gave

direction," says Phoebus,—"cease to do evil, learn to
do well; hear, read, and think of your latter end. Sinners ought to pray that their sins might be forgiven."

The following letter is an example of his counsel,
which he gave a friend:

Dear Sir,

I have looked over thine, which I received last Sabbath, as no answer was asked. I show thee a more excellent way: when men revile you and persecute you,
and say all manner of evil of you falsely, for Christ's
sake, 'rejoice and be exceeding glad; for great is your
reward in heaven.' 'Christ also suffered for us, leaving
us an example that we should follow his steps; who,
when he was reviled, reviled not again; when he suffered, threatened not; but committed himself to Him
that judgeth righteously.'

" 'Blessed is the man that endureth temptation; for
when he is tried, he shall receive the crown of life,
which the Lord, the righteous Judge, hath promised to
them that love Him.' Thy soul is more to thee than
all the churches in the world, and the government of
thy spirit, than all the disputes in Church and State!

Need I ask thee, whether thy soul is as happy as it
was before the separating Spirit was raised? As to
myself, I thank God that I am what I am.—May heavenly wisdom guide us through this world to the blissful regions of bright eternity.

Shall I say thine, the least of all the saints,

R. WHATCOAT.

Bishop Whatcoat was an expository preacher. Authority rested in a personal experience of God in life.
He substantiated this truth by Scriptural authority.
He knew the Scriptures as few ever did and was able
to quote and interpret them with power and effective-
ness.

Bishop Whatcoat's power as a preacher was the
result of a deep spiritual life. Rev. W. Thacher heard

him preach many times when he was stationed in New York, and said that he preached with peculiar unction, his word was attended with unusual power.

Dr. Boehm says, "Whatcoat excelled as a preacher. He could melt and mold an audience as few men ever did. The holy anointing rested on him and a peculiar unction attended his words. He was much of the spirit of the seraphic Fletcher." He further states that "never were holier hands laid upon a holier head."

Someone has said that "when he awoke in the night, he was in meditation or prayer, exulting and praising God like Paul and Silas, speaking to himself in spiritual songs, making melody in his heart with grace. This holy man was sent to the Church as if an example, to show to what a life of peace and holiness Christians may attain on earth."

William Phoebus adds that it might be said of him, as of St. Basil, "that so much divine majesty and luster appeared in him, it made the wicked tremble to behold him." Thus in him were seen majesty and love happily wedded as expressed by the following poem:

Shall I not again on earth behold
That countenance, so grave, so bold,
Which, with a look, could daunt the face of sin,
And make offence to hide itself within?
Most perfect image of the God above!
Without was majesty, within was love;
One drawn with sweetness by an infant's hand,
Not driven by violence, or base command.

Richard Whatcoat liked to preach the Gospel as revealed to him in mind and spirit. He gave himself wholly to this task, calculated to give expression to noble ideas and to inspire and influence souls with the true ideal for life.

Thanks to the human heart by which we live,
Thanks to its tenderness, its joys, its fears;
To me, the meanest flower that blows can give
Thoughts that do often be too deep for tears.

CHAPTER XIV.

THE MAN.

Whatcoat must have been especially attractive to the gentler sex, in manner, person, and moral purity; but he wrote, "God has enabled me to persevere in the work with a single eye. He has kept my heart disengaged from all creature loves, and all desire for worldly happiness. I can truly say: 'Blest with the scorn of finite good my soul is lightened of her load, and seeks the things above.'" Richard Whatcoat, like Francis Asbury, never married, yet he was wedded to the Bride of Christ—the Church.

Richard Whatcoat's personal appearance was interesting and inviting, and it pleased those about him. "The form of his body was competently genteel and grave," says William Phoebus; "his soul comprehensive, vigorous, noble, great, and active. His presence and aspect smooth and pleasant, yet solemn,—often striking reverence and awe into the minds and deportment of such as looked upon him, especially when exercising the office of his function."

"He was a refined gentleman," says Mains, "of purest life, unfaltering courage, and in labors abundant. His gentleness combined with firmness, his saintliness coupled with practical wisdom, his unremitting devotion to duty, all conspired to command for him the highest admiration and affection of his brethren."

"Such was his unabated charity," Asbury said in his funeral sermon, "his ardent love to God and man, his patience and resignation amid the unavoidable ills of life, that he always exemplified the tempers and conduct of a most devout servant of God and of an exemplary Christian minister."

William Phoebus makes a similar statement: "His amiable, heavenly, and courteous carriage was such as to make him the delight of his acquaintance, and to prepare them for the reception of his counsels and reproofs. His compassion for mankind in a lost condition, his acts of Charity to those in want—his tenderness for such as were culpable—his affectionate language and deportment in the exercise of his ministry, especially—and his love—were set forth in his ardent longings after the souls of his hearers. His rejoicing in their spiritual prosperity—his bleedings and heartbreakings for their backslidings—his labours among them, both public and from house to house—his frequent and affectionate letters to them when absent—his earnest desire to spend and be spent for them—always evinced what share they had in his affection."

"I think I may safely say," says Laban Clark, "if I ever knew one who came up to Saint John's description of a perfect man—one who bridled his tongue and kept in subjection his whole body—that man was Bishop Whatcoat."

Dr. Wakely says: "All who knew Richard Whatcoat attributed to him an uncommon degree of piety." Dr. Thomas E. Bond, Sr., said, "He was one of the purest spirits I ever knew. Everybody about the house loved him, cats, dogs, and all."

Mary Snethen remarked, "Of all the pure and holy men that came to that old parsonage, he seemed to be the most heavenly-minded. He talked of heaven, he sang of heaven, and meditated of heaven."

In November, 1806, Asbury wrote to Fleming: "Dear Father Whatcoat, after thirteen weeks' illness —gravel, stone, dysentery combined—died, a martyr to pain, in all patience and resignation to the will of

God. May we, like him, if we live long, live well, and die like him."

An old minister once said of Whatcoat: "I saw Richard Whatcoat in the old John Street parsonage. He sat there as if he saw no one, heard no one, and was in silent communion with God."

"For purity of character, for self-denial, for deep devotion, for heavenly-mindedness, for Divine unction, none of our preachers has ever surpassed him. What a name and influence he left behind, both fragrant and enduring."

Like Barnabas, "A good man, full of faith and the Holy Ghost."

> His soul disdain'd on earth to dwell
> He only sojourn'd here.

The Rev. Snethen says, "His life," as a pious young lady observed, "was like an even spun thread." We are also told that Richard Whatcoat had a second suit of natural hair, which Boehm tells us did not turn grey and "he never lost entirely his European color." His features were small and "after returning from the devotions of the closet, a painter or sculptor might have used him as a model for embodied sanctity." Mildness, complacency and dignity were so happily blended in his looks as to fill the beholder with reverence and love. His very appearance in the pulpit did his hearers good. Laban Clark describes him, at the New York conference, 1801, when he says, "I was charmed, not more with his simplicity and dignity of manners as presiding officer in the conference, than I was with his kind and cordial intercourse with the preachers out of it. He preached an excellent sermon on 'We glory in tribulations also,' etc., which was not

only adapted to all Christians, but especially appropriate to the young preachers who were then entering
the field of itinerant labor at a sacrifice which it is impossible now to esteem."

A New York official, in a letter to the Christian Advocate and Journal, 1828, regrets that so little notice
had been taken of such a superior man as Bishop
Whatcoat. "I traveled with him," and, says the writer,
"several times before and after he was made Bishop,
and a more upright and holy man I believe I never
saw."

The above statements may appear to the casual
reader that the portrait of Richard Whatcoat is over-
drawn. Yet to those who have known and studied his
life and work, it is all true. He was a man of forti-
tude; he feared not the face of man; he feared no
danger when duty called him, "believing that he who
walks uprightly, walks safely, though 'I walk through
the valley of the shadow of death, I will fear no evil;
for thou art with me; thy rod and thy staff they comfort me.'" Likewise, he never hesitated criticising
and condemning the wrong whenever and wherever he
saw it, but with much prudence, and with such expression of love and tenderness that it offended none.
but on the contrary, prepared their hearts and opened
the way more easily for the winning of their souls to
the Master.

All these facts have testified to his purity and
character as a man. There was another characteristic which I wish to mention here—his ability to work
out of difficult situations. This story is told by Dr.
Wakely in "The Lost Chapters" under the title "Whatcoat and the Lost Text." The story goes, "Mr. Whatcoat got into a great difficulty, but he showed himself a

genius in getting out of it, he announced his text and discoursed for a while, when his mind was drawn away from the subject, and he found it impossible to recall it. Said he, 'I have been talking so long, some of you may have forgotten the text,' he never hinted that he was in that category. 'Never mind if you have,' said he. 'I will take another.' He did so, and preached from it a most delightful sermon that was long remembered."

Richard Whatcoat was a man of peace, and a great peace-maker among his brethren wherever dissension arose from the lack of understanding, or from the lack of sober and peaceful principles.

He was a citizen of any country, state, city or hamlet. He esteemed the laws of the country, despising all unkindly expressions or unpatriotic actions. He kept a copy of the laws of the state wherever he was ministering, as a safeguard against the violation of its law. whereby the Gospel might be blamed. Likewise. we are told that he kept a manuscript of the municipal laws, whenever such could be obtained. so he might know how to conduct his services within the law.

A poem by William Wordsworth seems to be applicable to Whatcoat.

> Wide were his aims; yet in no human breast
> Could private feelings find a holier nest
> His joys, his griefs, have vanished like a cloud
> From Skiddaw's top; but he to heaven was vowed,
> Through a life long and pure and Christian faith
> Calmed in his soul the fear of change and death.

This was Richard Whatcoat the man. He was honest. frank, gentle, kind, and good. He could give reproof in such a way that it was never offensive. When Bishop Asbury broke out impetuously against the annoyance he suffered from too much company, Whatcoat mildly answered, "Oh, Bishop, how much worse we should feel, if we were entirely neglected." It is said that Bishop Asbury accepted the reproof and thanked his monitor for such a word in season.

Two days before his death, while he was being shaved, he became so full of joy and praise that the barber was forced to stop for a short time. He later explained that the cause of his emotion was that "he was thinking of the many pious and excellent people he had known in Europe and America and what a glorious time they would have when they all met in heaven." These last thoughts were not long unfulfilled. before Richard Whatcoat was escorted by The Arch Angel from the home of the Hon. Richard Bassett, Dover, Delaware, to the portals of his heavenly abode on July 5, 1806.

"And while we justly attribute to him," says Phoebus, "those qualities which constitute an 'able minister of the New Testament' we present, as the distinguishing trait of his character, a meekness and modesty of spirit which, united with a simplicity of intention and gravity of deportment, commended him to all as a pattern worthy of their imitation. So dear is he in the recollection of those who, from personal intercourse, best knew and appreciated his worth, that I have heard many such say, that they would give much could they possess themselves of a correct resemblance of him upon canvas. But as he has left no such likeness of himself behind, we must be content with offering this feeble tribute of respect to his memory, and then strive so to imitate his virtues that we may at last see him as he is, and unite with him in ascribing 'honor and dominion to him that sitteth upon the throne, and to the Lamb for ever.

The history of Methodism will never be complete until this staunch little Englishman, with ruddy face and gentle manner has been given his place along with Bishop Asbury in the laying of the foundation of American Methodism.

This is the man as his friends saw him. This is the man as we see him today. It is in such men that God seeks to reveal himself. What God was able to do through this devote and Christlike life he seeks to do through us in our day. Richard Whatcoat made the world a little better by having lived in it, so should we. "Lest we forget, lest we forget" this is our task.